NOW I KNOW WHY YOU LIKE BEING ON TOP! WHAT A VIEW!

Gravitation

Volume 2

By
Maki Murakami

TOKYOPOP
Los Angeles • Tokyo • London

Translator - Ray Yoshimoto
English Adaptation - Jamie S. Rich
Associate Editor - Paul Morrissey
Copy Editor - Bryce Coleman
Retouch and Lettering - Miyuki Ishihara
Cover Layout - Raymond Makowski

Editor - Jake Forbes
Managing Editor - Jill Freshney
Production Coordinator - Antonio DePietro
Production Managers - Jennifer Miller, Mutsumi Miyazaki
Art Director - Matt Alford
Editorial Director - Jeremy Ross
VP of Production - Ron Klamert
President & C.O.O. - John Parker
Publisher & C.E.O. - Stuart Levy

Email: editor@TOKYOPOP.com
Come visit us online at www.TOKYOPOP.com

A  Manga

TOKYOPOP Inc.
5900 Wilshire Blvd. Suite 2000
Los Angeles, CA 90036

Gravitation Vol. 2

ISBN: 1-59182-334-X

First TOKYOPOP® printing: October 2003

10 9 8 7 6 5 4
Printed in the USA

CONTENTS

THE MEMBERS OF THE GRAVITATION BAND

SHUICHI SHINDOU
A HIGH SCHOOL SENIOR, SHUICHI ONLY WANTS ONE THING IN LIFE—TO BE A ROCK STAR. HE'S THE LEAD SINGER OF THE BAND BAD LUCK. HIS SATINY VOICE AND TALENT FOR LYRICS HAVE GOT HIS FOOT IN THE DOOR, BUT THIS SOFT BOY WILL NEED THICKER SKIN TO MAKE IT IN THE DIRTY WORLD OF PROFESSIONAL MUSIC.
EIRI YUKI
A ROMANCE NOVELIST BY TRADE AND MUSIC CRITIC BY CIRCUMSTANCE. YUKI IS COLD AND ALOOF, AND HIS FLIPPANT CRITICISM OF SHUICHI'S LYRICS FORGES A TUMULTUOUS RELATIONSHIP THAT WILL FOREVER DRAW THE TWO MEN TOGETHER—WHETHER THEY LIKE IT OR NOT!
HIROSHI NAKANO
SHUICHI'S BEST FRIEND AND MUSICAL PARTNER IS THE GUITARIST FOR BAD LUCK. HE'S INCREDIBLY POPULAR AT SCHOOL, AND UNLIKE SHUICHI, HE'S A GOOD STUDENT TO BOOT.
MIKA SEGUCHI
EIRI YUKI'S SISTER. SHE'S MARRIED TO TOHMA SEGUCHI. SHE CONVINCED SHUICHI TO PRESSURE YUKI INTO TALKING TO HIS ESTRANGED FAMILY. IN EXCHANGE, SHE GAVE TOHMA BAD LUCK'S DEMO TAPE.
MAIKO SHINDOU
SHUICHI'S YOUNGER SISTER. SHE'S AN ACTIVE MEMBER OF THE SCHOOL'S STUDENT BODY. EVEN THOUGH SHE CONSTANTLY PICKS ON SHUICHI, SHE'S ALWAYS LOOKING OUT FOR HIS BEST INTERESTS.
TOHMA SEGUCHI
FORMERLY THE LEAD KEYBOARDIST FOR THE LEGENDARY BAND NITTLE GRASPER, HE'S NOW A PRODUCER AT N-G RECORDS. HE MANAGES THE BAND ASK AND HAS BEEN SCOUTING BAD LUCK AS A POTENTIAL NEW ACT.

STORY SO FAR...

SHUICHI SHINDOU IS DETERMINED TO BE A ROCK STAR—EVEN THOUGH HE HAS NO EXPERIENCE, UNTAPPED TALENT, AND NO BAND. AFTER FINDING A CHARISMATIC GUITARIST AND GETTING A GIG, HE'S READY TO SHOW THE WORLD HIS INGENIOUS LYRICS. SHUICHI IS CRUSHED WHEN NOVELIST EIRI YUKI SLAMS HIS AMATEURISH VERSE. UNABLE TO SHAKE THE HARSH CRITICISM, SHUICHI FORCES HIMSELF INTO YUKI'S LIFE, DESPERATE TO PROVE HIS MUSICAL PROWESS. THE TWO SUDDENLY FIND THEIR FUTURES INEXORABLY INTERTWINED. IS IT FATE? OR IS THIS FORCE SOMETHING MORE PRIMAL—LIKE GRAVITY?

track 5

EIRI!
WAKE UP, EIRI!
EIRI...
GRRRRRR
......
Stop playing dead!
shake
shake
shake
How cruel!!
You've tried this play a hundred times!
EIRI!!!
WAKE UP ALREADY!! YOU'RE THE WORST MORNING PERSON I'VE EVER SEEN!!
snooooore
....
....
...ASSHOLE.

ABOUT GRAVITATION TRACK 5

Ta da! We start off with Eiri in bed! Okay, I guess it's not that big of a deal. This episode, I had the nervous pleasure of drawing Eiri with a new haircut. It might not mean much to you, but now you get to see his nape for the first time. Nary a hair to be seen. What to do? I'm not sure how my readers will react - arousal, maybe? I'll bet no one cares that from Eiri's angle on the floor, he could probably steal a look at his sister Mika's panties. I hate saying it, but I'm really bad at drawing the female figure. Especially the legs. What is it with these legs? They look like columns of rock. It's around this episode that I decided to start revealing Tohma Seguchi's true colors. I splurged on the very first page and painted a lyrical background of white splashes, symbolizing the Milky Way. See how happy he looks? It's a picture that has a lot of meaning, reminding me of all the hard times I've given my editor...

......
she hit him again
YOU DON'T SAY?
OKAY.
THANKS. I GUESS.
Pillow
IT COULDN'T BE ABOUT WORK, COULD IT? IT MUST BE A HARD-KNOCK LIFE BEING A POPULAR NOVELIST.
OR IS IT A WAKE-UP CALL FULL OF SWEET NOTHINGS FROM A FEMALE EDITOR YOU'VE ALREADY BANGED?
smile
DO YOU REALLY THINK I'M DESPERATE ENOUGH TO SLEEP WITH MY EDITORS?
Now I'm awake, dammit!
ANYTHING'S POSSIBLE.
You punk!
ALL IT TAKES IS A SMALL FLASH OF CASH OR A RIDE IN ONE OF MY CARS...
...AND THE GIRLS LINE UP FOR MILES FOR A CHANCE TO SPEND THE NIGHT IN MY BED.
That's not necessary!

THEY'RE ALL SUPERFICIAL, EMPTY-HEADED BIMBOS. WITH TWO FACES.
ONE ON THEIR HEAD, ONE IN MY WALLET.
I CAN LEARN TO IGNORE IF SOMEONE IS STUPID.
DISHONESTY LINGERS LIKE A BAD SMELL.
IF I DIDN'T KNOW BETTER, I'D SAY YOU WERE TALKING ABOUT THAT SHINDOU KID.
Oh sweet Eiri... ♡
SHUT UP! THAT'S NOT WHAT I MEANT.
DON'T PRETEND YOU'RE SHY.
I said that's not what I meant!

BY THE WAY, WHERE IS HE?
WHO?
THE "GOOD SON," AS THE OLD MAN MIGHT CALL HIM.

OH, TATSUHA HAD TO GO OVER TO THE NEXT PREFECTURE TO PERFORM A MEMORIAL SERVICE.
Hmm ...
HE'S QUITE A PRIEST FOR BEING ONLY 16.
She's being decent enough to not watch while her brother changes.

AND QUITE A PLAYER, TOO.
I hear he's pretty promiscuous.

IT'S ALL IN THE SUPERIOR GENES. I'VE GOT THE OLD MAN TO THANK FOR THAT.
ha ha

I BELIEVE IT.
YOU GUYS ARE BROTHERS, AFTER ALL.

OH, WELL...
SAY HI TO HIM FOR ME.
WHERE ARE YOU GOING?
HOME.
Where's my lighter?
shuffle shuffle
Mika
WHAT?!
HOLD IT! WHAT DO YOU MEAN YOU'RE GOING HOME?!
Isn't it obvious?
I'VE BEEN HERE THREE DAYS ALREADY. ISN'T THAT ENOUGH?
I'M TOO BUSY TO PLAY FAMILY, AND FRANKLY, THIS PLACE IS BORING AS ALL HELL.

岡田総合病院
OKADA GENERAL HOSPITAL
IT'S JUST A SIMPLE COLD THAT'S BEEN AGGRAVATED BY STRESS AND LACK OF SLEEP.
I'M PRESCRIBING SOME PILLS FOR YOU, SO TAKE THOSE AND REST FOR TWO OR THREE DAYS.
YES...
THANK YOU VERY MUCH.
slap
USA
GIVEN THAT YOU ARE UP AND AROUND ALREADY, I THINK BRINGING YOU IN BY AMBULANCE WAS A BIT EXCESSIVE.
YOU SHOULD HAVE NOTHING TO WORRY ABOUT.
YOU'RE STILL YOUNG AND FULL OF ENERGY, AND THAT'LL WORK IN YOUR FAVOR.
Ha ha!

WHAT ?!
DON'T TOUCH
WHAT THE HELL HAPPENED HERE?!
POWER PC
ASR

NO COMPUTER GIZMOS FOR YOU UNTIL YOU'RE WELL!

She piled it on his bed
YOU CAN'T DO THIS!
OH, CAN'T I? YOU'RE JUST LUCKY I DON'T GIVE YOU A BEATING TO GO WITH YOUR COLD!
USA

YOU'RE BANNED FROM PLAYING YOUR KEYBOARD OR PLAYING AT NIGHTCLUBS UNTIL GRADUATION!
You didn't have to tape it all up like that...
WHAT ?!
I can't gig...?

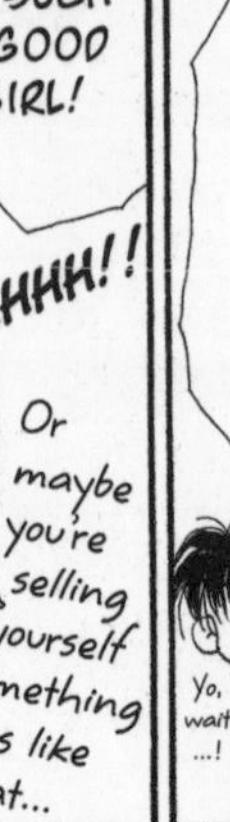

Wasn't that on the bed?

I CAN'T REALLY BLAME MOM FOR GETTING MAD...

Since all his equipment is on his bed, he's sleeping on the floor.

SIGH...

Medicine set

I PROBABLY DISRUPTED MIZUKI'S ENTIRE LIFE, TOO.

I SHOULDN'T GET SO DEPRESSED JUST BECAUSE MY AUDITION TAPE GOT TRASHED ONCE OR TWICE.

OR SO I THOUGHT...

ABOUT YOUR TAPE.
I'M SORRY, BUT...
TOHMA SAID HE DIDN'T NEED TO HEAR IT...
I KNEW I WAS BEING STUPID RIGHT FROM THE START.
BUT THEN AGAIN, MAYBE THERE'S NO SUCH THING AS LUCK OR COINCIDENCE.
MAYBE THIS IS REALITY.
BUT WHAT HURTS THE MOST...
...IS THAT I THREW AWAY THE BIGGEST CHANCE OF MY LIFE FOR SOMEONE ELSE.

THAT'S HOW MUCH...
IS THIS SHUICHI SHINDOU'S RESIDENCE?
Y-YES... SHUICHI IS MY SON.
...I WAS IN LOVE WITH HIM...
I'M SORRY FOR THE INTRUSION.
I'M A FRIEND OF SHUICHI'S. IT'S A PLEASURE TO MEET YOU.

I HEARD THAT HE WAS CONVALESCING AT HOME.
smile
I THOUGHT IT MIGHT CHEER HIM UP IF I PAID HIM A VISIT.
OH, ARE YOU A BAND MATE OF HIS OR SOMETHING?
WHY DON'T YOU COME IN?
THANK YOU VERY MUCH.
SOMETHING SMELLS REALLY NICE.
I GUESS THERE ARE STILL AROMAS IN YOUR DREAMS...

Wait a minute, aren't I awake...?
Then where's this fragrance coming from?
Hey.
Wake up, you little punk.
Huh?
むに
Hyu...
Hyuhi ?!
I figured you were dead.
That's no way to treat a guy.

* Y...Yuki?!

fwump
YIKES!
YOU SCARED ME!!
WHAT ARE YOU DOING HERE?!
cough
cough
YOU DON'T THINK IT'S FOR THE SCINTILLATING CONVER-SATION, DO YOU?
Or that I brought flowers? What am I? Stupid?
cough
UH... WELL, IT'S NOT THAT, BUT...
I WENT TO THE HOSPITAL AND THEY TOLD ME YOU HAD CHECKED OUT ALREADY.
SO I FIGURED YOU'D BE HERE.
WHAT?
Don't stare at me!
bedbug
UH...
UM... WELL...

I WAS LOOKING AT YOU TO ASK YOU...
...WHY YOU CAME TO SEE ME...?
in a tiny voice
BUT, YOU KNOW... WELL, NEVER MIND. THANKS FOR THE FLOWERS.
THEY, UH, THEY SMELL NICE. I COULD SMELL THEM EVEN IN MY DREAM...
YOU WANT TO KNOW WHY?
BECAUSE I WAS WORRIED ABOUT YOU, YOU MORON.

WHY THE HELL DID YOU TURN DOWN SEGUCHI?
ARE YOU DEFECTIVE OR SOMETHING? YOU PASS UP SOMETHING LIKE THAT JUST BECAUSE I YELLED AT YOU?
SO YOU WERE DEPRESSED AND YOU ENDED UP AT MIZUKI'S PLACE.
IF YOU DIED, THEN IT WOULD HAVE BEEN MY FAULT BECAUSE I FREAKED YOU OUT.
SHE CALLED ME AT MY PARENTS' PLACE TO TELL ME.
HUH?
Whatta bitch!
SO YOU DID GO HOME?! WHY?!
YOU'RE THE ONE WHO TOLD ME I SHOULD.

YEAH ...
THE BASTARD'LL PROBABLY LIVE ANOTHER THREE-HUNDRED YEARS.
That's great!
No, it isn't.

I NEVER DARED TO DREAM THAT YOU'D COME VISIT ME.
OR THAT I'D EVER BE GLAD I CAUGHT A COLD.
yayyy
SEGUCHI PROBABLY SLAMMED YOU BECAUSE HE SAW YOUR INNER IDIOT SHINING THROUGH.
Getting sick's a good thing?

snuggle
snuggle
I'M JUST TRYING TO PUT A HAPPY FACE ON IT.
mmph

I COULD GET REJECTED A THOUSAND TIMES...
...AND IT WOULD BE WORTH IT FOR YOU TO VISIT ME ONE TIME LIKE THIS.
pat
LOOK, KID...
HUH?
Mmm... This feels good.
WHAT IS IT ABOUT ME THAT YOU LIKE SO MUCH?

I DON'T REALLY BELIEVE THAT YOU'RE GAY. SO WHY ARE YOU COMING ON TO ME?
IS IT BECAUSE OF MY MONEY? MY LOOKS? I KNOW IT'S NOT FOR THE WITTY BANTER, UNLESS YOU'RE SOME KIND OF MASOCHIST.
NONE OF THAT MATTERS TO ME.
I DON'T UNDERSTAND IT MYSELF. I CAN'T HELP IT.
I CAN'T HELP BEING IN LOVE.
aah
......
ughh

KNOCK IT OFF ALREADY. YOU'RE GONNA GIVE ME YOUR COLD.
GO BACK TO BED.
NOOOOO!
Kya!
What are you, a turtle?
I DIDN'T SAY I WAS GOING ANYWHERE.
NO NO NO NO NO NO!
I don't wanna let go!
Dammit.
ALL RIGHT ALREADY!
W-WHOA!
YUKI...?!

IF YOU WANT IT THAT BAD, THEN WHO AM I TO DENY YOU?
LET'S DO IT.
WHAT?!
W- WAIT...
WAIT A MINUTE !!
grab
THAT'S NOT WHAT I MEANT... I WAS TALKING ABOUT--
STOP SQUIRMING AROUND OR I'LL HAVE TO GET ROUGH!
YOU'RE ALREADY ROUGH!!
Here we go.
WAIT A MINUTE! TIME OUT! MY MOM'S DOWN-STAIRS!
NO, SHE'S NOT.
WHAT ?!

SHE SAID SHE WAS GOING TO A SHINJI TANIMURA CONCERT WITH MS. FURUKAWA FROM NEXT DOOR, SO SHE ASKED ME TO BABYSIT YOU.
Please take care of Shuichi for me.
snore
A MOTHER'S LOVE, GOOD VIBES, YADDA YADDA YADDA! YEAH, RIGHT! IT'S ALL FAKE!!
Shuichi's head
SO, ANYWAY, YOU MAY AS WELL ENJOY YOURSELF.
HEY! WHAT ARE YOU DOING WITH YOUR HANDS?!
Having fun.
DON'T BE SUCH A WIMP.
ISN'T THIS WHAT YOU WANTED?

STOP IT,
YUKI...
GOD-
DAMMIT
...
THIS ISN'T
WHAT I
WANTED...
STOP
IT
!!!
NO...
STOP
IT!

WHY COULDN'T YOU JUST GIVE THE KID'S TAPE A LISTEN?
Okay.
Ok, Taki! It's about time you took
I MEAN, AFTER ALL, HE DID GO THROUGH THE PROPER CHANNELS TO GET IT TO YOU.
TURNING HIM AWAY LIKE THAT, AFTER HE MADE SUCH AN EFFORT, WAS A BIT CRUEL, DON'T YOU THINK?
All you need is keeping fine circumstances
I hope you break a leg!!
THAT AGAIN?!
YOU'RE RATHER STUBBORN TODAY, SAKANO.
WELL, IT'S JUST...
I THINK THE KID HAS POTENTIAL, SEGUCHI.

ASK
I THOUGHT SO THE MOMENT I SAW HIM PERFORMING.
SURE, HE'S STILL PRETTY ROUGH AROUND THE EDGES WHEN IT COMES TO SONGCRAFT...
...BUT I WAS IMPRESSED WITH HIS ENERGY AND COMMITMENT.
IT'S NOT SO MUCH HIS COMPOSING OR SINGING ABILITIES...
THERE'S SOMETHING POWERFUL ABOUT HIM THAT SUCKED ME IN. HE'S GOT CHARISMA.
....

SAKANO ....

UH, YEAH?!

HOW LONG HAVE YOU BEEN WORKING AS MY MANAGER?

peek

UH... WELL, LET'S SEE...

ABOUT THREE AND A HALF YEARS.

Uh-oh, he's pissed!

badum

badum

badum

I SEE.

THANK YOU FOR ALL OF YOUR HARD WORK.

You're a good man, Sakano.

WHAT?
WHEN WE'RE FINISHED WITH ASK, YOU CAN GO BACK TO JAPAN.
YOU'RE FIRED.

DUDE, BE A MAN. STOP CRYING LIKE A CHICK.
sob sob
IT'S NOT LIKE I EVEN GOT YOUR PANTS OFF.
I DIDN'T DO ANYTHING TO HURT YOU.
I'm the one who should be crying!
I DON'T BELIEVE THIS!
aaagh
I TOLD YOU TO STOP!
sob sob sob
You bawl like a little baby.
AND I DID! WHAT MORE DO YOU WANT?
Aren't you a grown-up yet?

Ma-
Masochist punk?!
I-I COULDN'T HELP IT...
IT FELT... WELL...
...NICE...
か
blush...
AW, MAN...
You idiot!
GRRRRRR
WHAT AM I DOING WITH A LITTLE KID LIKE YOU ANYWAY?!

GRRRR
WHADDYA HAVE TO SAY THAT FOR?!
YOU'RE THE ONE WHO ATTACKED ME!
SO ARE YOU HAPPY NOW?
I THINK WE'RE EVEN.
I VISITED MY FATHER LIKE YOU ASKED ME TOO...
...AND THEN I EVEN CAME TO VISIT YOU.
SO DON'T EVER MAKE STUPID EXCUSES TO SEE ME ANYMORE!
Being blunt.
ガーん
WHA--?

WAAAAHHHHHH

WHAT?!

TWINGE

WHAT THE HELL DO YOU MEAN?! DON'T EVER SEE YOU AGAIN?! YOU'RE SAYING IT LIKE IT'S ALL MY FAULT!

That's too much!

YOU CAN'T STOP ME! I WANT TO SEE YOU NO MATTER WHAT!

THAT'S NOT WHAT I MEANT, YOU DUMBASS.

gyaaaaa

You're freaking me out.

I MEAN THAT YOU CAN COME SEE ME...

...WITHOUT HAVING TO MAKE UP SOME LAME STORY.

JUST DON'T GET ANY FUNNY IDEAS.
hmph
I'M NOT LIKE YOU. I'M STRAIGHT, OKAY?
......
......
shuttle shuttle shuttle shuttle
backed against the wall
ALL RIGHT ALREADY! STOP HANGING ALL OVER ME!
GYAAAAA!
YOU'RE GONNA GET YOUR COLD COOTIES ON ME!
What the hell's wrong with you?!
YOU'RE ONE WEIRD KID, YOU KNOW THAT?

IF YOU DON'T WANT MONEY OR SEX, THEN WHAT IS IT YOU WANT FROM ME?
I'M MEAN AND CRUEL, SO WHY HANG AROUND ME?
just collapsed from fever
mmph
"I CAN'T HELP BEING IN LOVE"?
NOT EVEN MY ROMANCE NOVELS ARE THAT BAD.
IS THAT WHAT LOVE IS?
SOME STUPID CLICHÉ?

3-B
WHAAAAAT?!
YOU MEAN THE GUY MOM SAID "LOOKED JUST LIKE EIRI YUKI AND WAS SO HANDSOME AND POLITE THAT I COULD NEVER IMAGINE THAT HE HAD ANYTHING TO DO WITH A BAND SO I ENDED UP ASKING HIM TO BABYSIT YOU"...
THAT GUY WAS THE REAL EIRI YUKI?!
UH...
WELL... YEAH...

W-
WHY...?
WHY COULDN'T YOU MAKE HIM STAY UNTIL I GOT BACK HOME?! SELFISH DICKHEAD!
Give me back my bento!
WELL...! I COULDN'T HELP IT! I HAD A FEVER AND I THOUGHT I WAS GONNA DIE!
Distress!
you idiot!
Rock
You traitor! Die!
WHEN YOUR BUDDIES ARE HARD AT WORK AT SCHOOL, YOU'RE SITTING AROUND LIVING THE HIGH LIFE!
You ain't hard at work!
(well, I doubt it ♡)
Head
YOU GOTTA KEEP THIS A SECRET! DON'T TELL ANYONE, OKAY?!
WHAT? WHY?
MY OWN BIG BROTHER IS IN AN INTIMATE RELATIONSHIP WITH EIRI YUKI. ♡
HOW CAN I NOT MAKE THIS INFORMATION PUBLIC? ♡
tra la la
art direction
COME ON...

whisper
I'M HAVING A HARD ENOUGH TIME IN SCHOOL AS IT IS!
whisper
IF RUMOR GETS OUT THAT ME AND EIRI YUKI HAVE SOME KIND OF QUESTIONABLE FRIENDSHIP...
This really sucks!

WHAT ARE YOU WORRIED ABOUT? YOU'RE GONNA FAIL ANYWAY.
Heh.
DON'T SAY THAT!
Shuichi!
Whaddya mean, "Heh"?
It's morning break time.
COME ON. I TRUSTED YOU GUYS, THAT'S WHY I TOLD YOU.
Especially you, Maiko!
Okay... THEN YOU HAVE TO PAY ME TO KEEP MY MOUTH SHUT.
I'll buy you the new Eiri Yuki novel when it comes out.

SO? SO? ARE YOU GOING TO GO ON A DATE SOON?
Big brother! I want to meet Eiri Yuki-sama!
WE'RE NOT DATING.

GUESS WHAT?

TODAY I'M GOING TO STUDY ANCIENT HISTORY AT HIROSHI'S PLACE!!

YOU MEAN YOU'RE GOING TO COPY ALL OF MY NOTES.

Hey, that's my breakfast!

WHAT?! MY BIG BROTHER IS GOING TO STUDY?

IS HE THAT DEEP IN TROUBLE?!

NO.

IT'S JUST THAT MOM LOCKED AWAY MY MUSICAL EQUIPMENT AND I'VE GOT NOTHING ELSE TO DO WITH MY TIME.

I SHOULD'VE KNOWN!

Fender STRATOCASTER

I'M SORRY.

I SHOULD'VE VISITED YOU WHILE YOU WERE SICK.

HM? OH, DON'T WORRY ABOUT IT.

REALLY? I GOT THE FEELING YOU WERE PISSED.

Oh, yeah, you bet I am!

Pick

hmmm

WHICH COLLEGE ARE YOU TRYING FOR?

BOKOKURITSU MEDICAL SCHOOL.

MED SCHOOL?!
YOU'RE GONNA BE A DOCTOR?!
YEAH.
whoa! I don't believe it!
THAT'S COOL, MAN. A DOCTOR BY DAY, GUITARIST BY NIGHT.
THERE'S NO WAY I'LL HAVE TIME TO PULL THAT OFF.
SORRY.
I'M GOING TO QUIT PLAYING.
...
WHAT--?

DON'T...
...JOKE AROUND, MAN.
HIRO?
I'VE ALREADY DECIDED.
I'M THROUGH WITH MUSIC.
track5▶END

Gravitation

track 6

DON'T WORRY. YOU'LL FIND A NEW PARTNER NO PROBLEM.
YOU'RE QUITTING THE BAND?!
WHY?!
DID I DO SOMETHING TO MAKE YOU MAD...?!

ABOUT GRAVITATION TRACK 6

Hiro -- A long-haired guitarist whose best friend is always giving his parents fits, Hiro is actually a superb student. (That's one hell of a character description there, eh?) He exudes the kind of aura that makes you believe he's capable of just about anything, but to be honest, even now, I haven't quite gotten his movements and speech patterns down yet. Hiroshi Nakano. It's usually nice guys like these that surprise you one day by doing something completely off the wall. (But that's just my personal opinion!) He's the kind of guy who, without realizing there is a passionate person inside him, goes through everyday life with ease and little fanfare. I'd like to make an analogy—he's like a civic hall with an undetonated bomb buried inside. He's the kind of guy that makes you think he's capable of something incredible, whether he's done anything or not. I really like this mysterious character of Hiro. A very nice guy. But beneath his gentle exterior lies a more dangerous side... If you were ever looking to date any of the Gravitation characters, I'd recommend Hiro in a second. I can guarantee you an exciting high school romance with this guy. When you finish reading this chapter, I'm sure you'll be under his spell, too.

ガチャ
WHAT'S ALL THE RACKET?!
HIRO! ARE YOU GUYS FIGHTING?!
IT'S NOTHING, MOM.
WE WERE JUST DISCUSSING PRIME MINISTER HASHIMOTO'S POSITION ON THE HOUSING LOAN SITUATION, AND YOU KNOW HOW HEATED I GET WHEN IT COMES TO POLITICS!
ばっ
Right? ♡

REALLY? I THOUGHT I HEARD YOU TALKING ABOUT YOUR GUITAR PLAYING...
HIRO, YOU'RE NOT THINKING OF STARTING THE GUITAR AGAIN, ARE YOU? I THOUGHT WE SETTLED THAT.
YOUR EXAMS ARE JUST AROUND THE CORNER. YOU HAVE TO BE READY.

WELL, THERE YOU GO...
I GUESS MY PARENTS SEE ME AS THE LAST HOPE FOR THE FAMILY.
MY BROTHER WANTS TO BE AN ACTOR, BUT HE HASN'T GOTTEN ANY PARTS, JUST ODD JOBS.
HE PROBABLY SHOULD PACK IT IN, SINCE HE'S NOT VERY GOOD.
HE'S GETTING OLD, AND IT JUST AIN'T HAPPENING.
I DON'T WANT A LIFE LIKE THAT.
IF YOU WANT TO SAY I'M SELLING OUT, GO RIGHT AHEAD.
I CAN'T HELP IT. I WANT AN EASY LIFE.

YOU CAN'T EAT A DREAM, BUT REALITY PUTS FOOD ON THE TABLE.
twinge
THE MUSIC'S OVER.

ARE YOU LISTENING TO YOURSELF?
IS THAT HOW LITTLE THE MUSIC MEANT TO YOU?
WHAT ABOUT OUR FRIENDSHIP? THE HOURS... YEARS! ...WE SPENT PLAYING TOGETHER.
I'M SORRY...

A bureaucrat in the making!

I'M SURE NAKANO AND YOUR BROTHER ARE LOOKING TO BECOME BIG MUSIC STARS, RIGHT?
WELL... YOU SEE...
IT'S NOT LIKE THAT...
NOT ANYMORE.
3 - B
G'MORNING ...
eh
whoa
どわあ
SHINDOU!
WHAT HAPPENED?! DID YOU AND NAKANO GET IN A FIGHT?!
AREN'T YOU GONNA DO ANYTHING FOR GRADUATION ?!

YOU GUYS ARE THE ONLY PART I'M LOOKING FORWARD TO!!

THE ENTIRE CLASS HAS BEEN WAITING ALL YEAR TO SEE YOU AND NAKANO SEND THINGS OFF WITH A BANG!!

YOU NO LONGER HAVE A CHOICE IN THE MATTER! YOU'VE GOTTA TALK NAKANO INTO DOING IT!! OR WE'LL BURN THE PLACE DOWN!

DO YOU EVER SHUT UP?

I CAN'T STUDY WITH YOU GUYS MAKING ALL THAT NOISE.

IT'S TOO EARLY IN THE MORNING FOR THAT CRAP.

PUNK

Okay okay.
I GUESS WE CAN'T DISTURB THE FUTURE MED STUDENT, NOW, CAN WE?
FORGIVE US, HERR DOKTOR!!
むっ
GRRRRRR
Forget it, man.
WELL, LA-DEE-DA! IT'S ALL CRAP TO HIROSHI!
M.D. MUST MEAN MAJORLY DAMAGED! YOU CAN'T BE SEEN WITH THE COMMON PEOPLE LIKE US!
Wow, he's lost it!
silence
YOU'RE ALWAYS THE SAME, MAN! SOON AS YOU GET BORED WITH SOMETHING, YOU COMPLETELY COP OUT!!
IF OUR MUSIC MEANT SO LITTLE TO YOU, THEN YOU MUST BE RIGHT--IT IS ALL CRAP!

EEEEEK!
WHOA! YO, NAKANO...
It's a fight!
I'M SICK OF YOUR SHIT!! WHAT MAKES YOU SO HIGH AND MIGHTY?
OWW
I SAID I'M QUITTING! SO WHAT? LEAVE ME ALONE!!

FINE! I'LL LEAVE YOU ALONE!!
STUDY YOUR LIFE AWAY IN MED SCHOOL, YOU PUSSY!
BABY BOY BETTER NOT DISAPPOINT HIS MOMMY!!
FINE!
I'LL DO WHAT I WANT!
THERE'S A MILLION GUITARISTS WITH WAY MORE TALENT THAN YOU!
FIGHT! FIGHT!
YOU WERE THE ONE WHO KEPT BEGGING ME TO PLAY IN YOUR STUPID BAND!!
HEY...
WHAT THE HELL DO YOU THINK YOU'RE DOING?!
Help!
Math Made Fun

GO TO HELL!
STOP IT! STOP IT, SHINDOU!!
YOU'RE JUST RUNNING AWAY, YOU COWARD!!
HOW CAN YOU CALL YOURSELF MY BEST FRIEND?!
NAKANO HAS TO GET READY FOR HIS SECOND TERM EXAMS NEXT MONTH!!
Yeah, tell him, teach'!
Teacher's working hard!
GRRR
DO YOU WANT HIM TO FAIL BECAUSE OF YOU?!
HE'S NOT LIKE YOU, SHINDOU!
LEAVE HIM ALONE!!

You got that right!!
HIRO'S NOT LIKE ME! HE'S AN "A" STUDENT!!
TEACHER'S PET CAN'T BE WASTING HIS TIME PLAYING GUITAR!!
NO...
THAT'S NOT TRUE...
He got bounced.
Aw, man.

GO HOME!
NO.
I CAN'T GO BACK TO MY PLACE LOOKING LIKE THIS.
crumble
LISTEN... SURE, I DID TELL YOU THAT YOU COULD COME OVER ANYTIME...
GRRRRR
Wait a minute, did they gang bang you in gym class or something?
STOP GROWLING, YOU FREAK.
GRRRR RRRRRR
......

HIRO? YOU MEAN YOUR GUITARIST FRIEND?
YEAH.
DUNK
hmph
These bandages never used before!
THEY SAY IT TAKES GOOD FRIENDS TO HAVE A GOOD FIGHT, BUT THIS IS RIDICULOUS.
BUT HE STARTED IT!!
AAGH!
DON'T YELL! I'VE BEEN UP FOR OVER TWO DAYS STRAIGHT TRYING TO MAKE A DEADLINE!
I... I'M SORRY...
IF YOU HAVE TO APOLOGIZE, THEN DON'T DO IT, PUNK.
DUNK

YOU WANT COFFEE? TEA? BEER? MILK? WATER?
Water?
NO THANKS...
OKAY.
どすん
tick tock tick tock tick tock tick tock tick
badum badum badum badum badum
IF YOU CHANGE YOUR MIND AND WANT SOMETHING...
...LET ME KNOW.

Time's running out. 5... 4... 3...
...2...
Uh...
C-could you k-k-kiss...
...m-m--
ki...
...1.
Zero. Time's up. Too bad.
bzzzzzzzt
Wotta comedian!
......
Hold on a minute!!
ARGGGGGHHHH
All right already! AAAAGH
I said it at 2! I said it at 2!!
I said it at 2! I wanna kiss!!
Okay then. COME HERE!
Grab

MMPH--
COME ON. OPEN YOUR MOUTH.
ISN'T THIS WHAT YOU WANTED?
MM!
GRAB
GYAAA
HEY!
WAAA AHHHH! YUKI!!

WHA...?
WHAT'S THE MATTER?! GOD!
Man, you scared me!
WAAAHHHH
WHAT AM I GONNA DO?!
I'm gonna fall!
WAHHHHH
sob
I...I WAS SO MEAN TO HIRO...
I KNOW HE HATES ME NOW...
WHAT AM I GOING TO DO WITHOUT HIM?!
......
I KNOW HE REALLY WANTS TO KEEP PLAYING GUITAR, BUT SINCE HIS BROTHER... AND HIS PARENTS...
HE CAN'T DO ANYTHING ABOUT IT...IT SUCKS...
sob
I TOLD HIM HE WASN'T MY BEST FRIEND ANYMORE.
sob

WHAT ARE YOU CRYING ABOUT?
Huh?
HE REALLY LOVES PLAYING THE GUITAR, RIGHT?
sob, hic
NNGHH Uh-huh.
wipe
Sniffle
THEN HE'S BEING AN IDIOT.
YOU SHOULDN'T BLAME YOURSELF.
BUT...
YOU'VE GOT TOO MUCH GUTS FOR HIM. YOU DO WHAT YOU WANT. LIKE HOW YOU CAN FALL IN LOVE WITH SOMEBODY AND NOT WORRY ABOUT SEXUALITY.
Ah, finally you stop crying!

IF I WERE HIRO, I'D TRY TO BE A BIT STRONGER AND MORE PIGHEADED--LIKE YOU.
AND IT'S NEVER EVEN CROSSED YOUR MIND THAT I MAY NOT WANT YOUR ATTENTION, HAS IT?
WELL, YEAH... BUT...
I REALLY SAID SOME TERRIBLE THINGS TO...
...UMM--
Yukiiiii!!!
Aaaaagh!
marble table

H-HEY! ARE YOU ALL RIGHT?!
Don't die on me! Wake up!
You're asleep?!
YUKI... I...
ZZZ ZZZ
※Table
......
Blush
H-HE'S KINDA...CUTE, Y'KNOW...ALL THINGS CONSIDERED...
Eiri's jaw
I'M NOT STRONG AT ALL...
C'mon, Yuki, get up!
Goddammit! Get up, you prick!
huff huff huff
DAMN, HE WON'T WAKE UP.
I'M ABSOLUTELY AFRAID OF FACING REALITY.
YOU'RE KIND OF FREAKING ME OUT, MAN.
ZZZzz

IT'S EASY FOR ME TO BE SELFISH AND TELL HIRO HE'S WRONG...
...BUT IT'S PROBABLY BETTER FOR HIM TO BE A DOCTOR THAN TO HANG AROUND WITH ME.
BUT...
THE REASON I CAN PURSUE SOMETHING WITH NO FEAR...
If you don't get up, I'm gonna rape you!
NO MATTER HOW MUCH I NEED HIRO...
...IS BECAUSE I'M AFRAID TO GO WITHOUT IT.
NOTHING HURTS QUITE LIKE...
...UNREQUITED LOVE.
...HE PROBABLY DOESN'T NEED ME AT ALL.
THAT'S WHAT SCARES ME THE MOST.

HIROSHI!
Heyyyyyy
うりば
......
ha ha ha
HEY.
WHAT ARE YOU DOING HERE, YUJI?
I'M HERE TO PICK YOU UP, BRO. ♡
Hm?

HOW'S IT HANGIN'?
YOU TAKE YOUR TESTS ALREADY? ACE `EM?
NOPE. I TANKED.
HA HA HA. ALL YOU NERDS SAY THE SAME THING, AND YOU ALL PASS ANYWAY.
I CAN'T BELIEVE MY LITTLE BROTHER IS GONNA BE A DOCTOR.
DON'T COUNT ON IT.
smile
DON'T BE SO DRAMATIC, KIDDO. YOU'LL BE FINE!
I'M NOT FINE! EVEN IF I HAD KNOWN ANY OF THE ANSWERS, IT WOULDN'T HAVE MATTERED BECAUSE I SLEPT THROUGH THE ENTIRE TEST!
...

IS THAT BITTERNESS I HEAR? YOU SINK ANOTHER AUDITION?
Not that you seem stressed or anything.
LIKE A FREAKIN' STONE! EIGHTEEN FACE PLANTS IN A ROW! A NEW RECORD! WOO!
ha ha ha ha ha ha ha ha
ha ha ha ha
WELL, AT LEAST IT'S OVER.
I WOULDN'T WORRY ABOUT IT. THINGS TEND TO WORK THEMSELVES OUT FOR LUCKY BASTARDS LIKE YOU.
smile
DON'T YOU EVER GET DEPRESSED OR EVEN ASK YOURSELF WHY?
YOU'LL NEVER GET HIRED IF YOU KEEP THIS UP.
You know?
YEAH, MAYBE, I SUPPOSE.
BUT WHAT DO I CARE?
I'M HAVING A GOOD TIME. ♡

MOM AND DAD ARE PRETTY UPSET.
YOU'VE BEEN GOING NOWHERE FOR FIVE YEARS, AND YOU'RE STILL SINGLE AT 23!
WHO CARES WHAT OUR PARENTS THINK? MY LIFE IS MY LIFE, AND I'M HAPPY.
IF ALL YOU CARE ABOUT IS THE CORPORATE LADDER AND TAKING THE SAFE ROUTE, YOU'LL NEVER HAVE ANY FUN.
I MAY FAIL EVERY TIME I DO SOMETHING, BUT AT LEAST IT'S INTERESTING.
HOW DID HE GET THIS WAY?
HE DOESN'T HAVE ANY FEAR. HE NEVER HESITATES AND NEVER FROWNS.
JUST LIKE SHUICHI...
Hey!
WHAT'S THE MATTER, HIROSHI? YOU LOOK BUMMED. YOU HUNGRY?

YOU ALWAYS SEEM SO HAPPY.
Even when you eat.
HAVE YOU EVER THOUGHT ABOUT THE FUTURE? EVEN ONCE?
That's pretty harsh!
YOU JUST THINK I'M SOME BIG LOSER, DON'T YOU?
Maybe I am, I guess.
NO, THAT'S NOT WHAT I MEANT.
I JUST WONDERED HOW YOU COULD BE SO HAPPY. THAT'S ALL.
NOBODY COULD BE UNHAPPY DOING WHAT THEY LOVE.
heh

What's that mean?
WELL, YEAH... I SUPPOSE SO...
BUT TO MOST PEOPLE, YOU'VE HIT ROCK BOTTOM...
THERE'S NO GUARANTEE YOU'LL EVER ACHIEVE YOUR DREAMS, AND YOU HAVE TO WORK EVERY DAY AT SOME LAMEASS JOB TO SURVIVE.
IF EVERYTHING WAS EASY, THERE'D BE NO POINT DOING IT.
IF DREAMS WERE SIMPLE, EVERYONE WOULD LIVE THEIRS.
FOR A LOSER, YOU SEEM TO BE HOLDING ALL THE CARDS.
sip
I PLAY WHAT I'M DEALT.
IS IT STUPIDITY ...
...OR STRENGTH?

AS A KID...

...I ALWAYS WANTED TO BE AS STRONG AS YOU.

HAVE A LITTLE FAITH IN YOURSELF AND YOUR DESIRES.
THERE'S ALWAYS TIME TO RUN AWAY LATER.
I GUESS...
...I MUST BE A LOUSY BEST FRIEND.
IF YOU EVER START TO MOPE AGAIN AND DOUBT YOURSELF, I'LL BE HERE TO SET YOU STRAIGHT.
I MAY BE A LAMEASS LOSER...
...BUT I'M STILL YOUR BIG BROTHER.
heh
NO WONDER YOU CAN'T GET A GIG!
YOUR DELIVERY IS TERRIBLE!

I CAN'T BELIEVE IT'S GRADUATION ALREADY!
SO, DID YOUR BROTHER AND HIS BOYFRIEND MAKE UP?
Mr. President, we've finished the pamphlets for the sophomore class.
Okay, hand them to Mr. Yamada.
DON'T BE A DICK.
AND THE ANSWER'S "NO."
phewww
CLASSES ARE ALREADY FINISHED FOR THE SENIORS.
THEY'VE HAD NO REASON TO END THEIR COLD WAR.
I TAKE IT YOUR SPASTIC SIBLING DOESN'T KNOW, THEN, EH?
THEY ANNOUNCED THE TEST RESULTS FOR NAKANO'S COLLEGE ENTRANCE EXAMS.
GRADUATIO Program
....

I WANTED TO CELEBRATE NAKANO'S GRADUATION WITH A BIG BANG...

...BUT I'M AFRAID IT MIGHT JUST BE A WHIMPER.

AND NOW, TO REPRESENT THE GRADUATING CLASS...

...FROM HOMEROOM B...

HIRO...

...THE GRADUATING SPEAKER, HIROSHI NAKANO.

I WANT SO BADLY TO APOLOGIZE TO YOU.
EVEN IF WE GO OUR SEPARATE WAYS...
...YOU'RE STILL MY BEST FRIEND.
Nakano! Please don't leave us!
eee! eee!
Quiet please!
I'M GOING TO TELL YOU HOW I FEEL.
sob
FELLOW STUDENTS, OUR INVITED GUESTS...
TELL YOU WHAT A GREAT DOCTOR YOU'LL BE...
I FAILED MY ENTRANCE EXAM.
silence

EVEN WORSE THAN THAT...
...I ALSO FAILED AS A BEST FRIEND.
I FAILED MY DREAMS.
I HOPE YOU'LL STILL LET ME BE YOUR GUITARIST.
SHUICHI.
Why do I always end up with these losers in my class?!
Gyaaaaa
Weirdest commencement address ever!
N-NAKANO!! WHAT THE HELL ARE YOU...?
!!
!!

S-
SHINDOU?! HOLD ON, DON'T--!!
AAAAAGHHH
Calm down, Mr. Takimura!
You can hit him all you want after it's over! Let's let the ceremony end peacefully!

I'M SORRY.

PAT
CONGRATU-
LATIONS!
IT'S A
SPLENDID
FAILURE!
WHOOO
THANK
YOU!
OOSK!
THAT WAS
CERTAINLY
...UH...SOME
SPEECH!

BAMMMMM
どーーん
FOR THE NEXT PART OF OUR EVENT...
MY DARLING BOYFRIEND IS PUTTING HIS STUDENT BODY PRESIDENT ASS ON THE LINE HERE! YOU BETTER MAKE THIS A GOOD ONE!
...WE HAVE A SURPRISE! A SPECIAL LIVE REUNION OF THE SCHOOL'S COOLEST BAND!
You've gotta be kidding!
Hey, big bro!
Executive Committee
YAAAAAAAHHHH
おおおー
Darling!
ALL RIGHT!
MAIKO...
Whatta school this is!
IS THIS A GOOD IDEA? I'M OUT OF PRACTICE. I HAVEN'T PLAYED FOR WEEKS.
rip
YEAH, MY MOM TOOK MY KEYBOARD AWAY, TOO!
ガン
I GUESS WE'RE BOTH FREE TO JAM ALL WE WANT, NOW.
ガン
IT LOOKS LIKE OUR FRIENDSHIP IS NO LONGER ON HOLD, EITHER.
ガン
ばりっ
WELL, THEN...
making room

Beep
BANZAI
LADIES AND GENTLEMEN!
LET'S GIVE HIROSHI A HAND FOR SO EXCELLENTLY FAILING HIS EXAM! BANZAI!!
Don't we have any good students at this school?
EEE!
Hey, thanks everyone!
ha ha ha
AND NEXT ...
...WE CELEBRATE YOU LOWERING YOUR GOALS!
YES, MASTER! ♡
BLINGGGGGG
M-MY H-HIRO...
All right then! You ready to rock?!
HMM.
I'LL SAY THIS, THEY ARE DIFFERENT.

YAAAAAAAH
Congratu-
lations for
what?!
YOUR SON?
CONGRATU-
LATIONS!
HEY! ONE
OF THOSE
IS MY SON!
WHAT ARE
YOU
IMPLYING?
eeek
DON'T
WORRY.
EVERYTHING'S
WORKING OUT
FINE.
OH,
HIRO
!!!
WAHHHHHH
clap
clap
clap

20/20 vision
?
HEY,
IS THAT YUKI'S SISTER?
Why are all of you clapping?! It's terrible!
OKAY!
スッ
clap
clap
clap
HEY, YOU TWO...

THIS GUY AGAIN...?
HOW'D YOU LIKE TO MAKE A RECORD?
track6▶END

Gravitation
track 7

WHAT THE HELL?
WHAT DOES HE MEAN?
IS HE SERIOUS ABOUT MAKING A RECORD?
IS THIS GUY REALLY FOR REAL?!

I'M SORRY FOR CRASHING YOUR GRADUATION YESTERDAY.
phew
I ARRIVED FROM NEW YORK AT SIX IN THE MORNING, AND I WAS PRETTY TIRED.
I WANTED TO GO HOME, BUT FOR SOME REASON MRS. SEGUCHI WAS WAITING FOR ME IN BAGGAGE CLAIM AT NARITA AIRPORT.
She was holding my luggage hostage.
Hey, those're my bags!
Tee-hee, if you want 'em back, come with me!
Baggage Claim
Sakano
Sakano
N-G CORP
SHE SAID SHE WANTED TO SHOW ME SOMETHING INTERESTING.
WE ENDED UP AT TOHOKU HIGH SCHOOL, WHICH WAS KIND OF A SURPRISE.
I thought she was going to eat me alive!
I don't understand why Seguchi-san married such a ballbuster.
I think I would have made a better housewife...
I DON'T GET IT...
You think you'd make a better housewife?

ABOUT GRAVITATION TRACK 7

Their first time. The day has finally come.
I've thought about how I'd handle this moment ever since I started the first chapter. "I know the day will come. I will make it happen." I never thought it would take seven chapters for us to get here, though. There are a lot of things I wish I had done differently, but I feel a sense of accomplishment now that I've completed it—so, it's been a happy chapter for me. Somehow I feel a bit light-headed now. Something that's starting to bug me, though—Sakano's messy hair in the scene where he's drinking tea.

WELL, REGARDLESS...
I WASN'T KIDDING WHEN I SAID I WANTED TO MAKE A CD WITH YOU.
I THINK IT'D BE GREAT.

YOU KNOW...
WHEN YOU AND SEGUCHI FIRST CAME TO SEE US PLAY...
Seguchi-san, are you tired? Do you need a coat? Are you thirsty? Would you like some coffee?
Seguchi-san, I arranged a car.
Sakano, that's all fine, but Shindou here is about to die of blood loss...
Gravitation Book 1, p.107, three minutes later
...I THOUGHT THAT YOU WERE HIS MANAGER, THE WAY YOU WERE MAKING EVERYTHING HAPPEN...

WELL, THAT'S BECAUSE I WAS.
HUH? HOW DID YOU GO FROM MANAGER TO PRODUCER?

WELL, I WAS FIRED AS MANAGER.
WHICH KIND OF MAKES ME WONDER HOW GOOD A PRODUCER YOU ARE... y'know?

ARE YOU DISAPPOINTED THAT IT'S ME AND NOT SEGUCHI?
IS THAT IT, SHUICHI?

NO!
O-OF...OF COURSE NOT!!
twinge
CLATTER
TO GET SUCH AN OFFER FROM MY IDOLS N-G, I'M MORE THAN HAPPY!
I'M INCREDIBLY HAPPY! ECSTATIC, EVEN!
I'M SUCH A BIG FAN OF NITTLE GRASPER!
I know I am overdoing it, yes...!
THEIR MUSIC INSPIRES ME TO THIS DAY! I DON'T CARE IF THEY BROKE UP! PURPLE NURPLE IS MY FAVORITE ALBUM!
WHEN SEGUCHI WENT SOLO, IT MADE MY OWN PATH CLEAR. I KNEW THERE WAS NO OTHER WAY INTO THE MUSIC BUSINESS FOR ME. I HAD TO DO IT WITH N-G!
GETTING SCOUTED BY YOU GUYS HAS BEEN MY ULTIMATE FANTASY!
I'M SO STOKED I COULD SPURT BLOOD FROM MY EVERY PORE! LIKE I WAS ONE BIG PIMPLE!
blood
Uh...
DON'T WORRY. HE'LL CALM DOWN. YOU JUST GOT TO LET HIM GET THINGS OUT OF HIS SYSTEM.
Just think of him as a roller coaster. The first time is rough, but you'll get used to it. Probably.
But...

OKAY ...
I THINK WE'RE ON THE SAME PAGE. WE ALL WANT TO MAKE THIS ALBUM.
NOW IT'S JUST A MATTER OF HASHING OUT THE REALITIES.

I'VE ONLY SEEN YOU PLAY ONCE, BUT I KNOW YOUR DEMO PRETTY WELL.
DOES SHINDOU DO ALL THE WRITING AND ARRANGING?
?
YES...

HOW WOULD YOU FEEL IF I TOLD YOU TO FOCUS EXCLUSIVELY ON YOUR VOCALS?

WHAT ...?
DON'T GET ME WRONG, THE WRITING ISN'T BAD.
IT'S JUST WHEN I SAY NOT BAD, I MEAN FOR AN AMATEUR. IT'S NOWHERE NEAR A PROFESSIONAL LEVEL.

N-G IS IN THE MUSIC BUSINESS, AND OUR MISSION IS TO PRODUCE PLATINUM-SELLING RECORDS.
FROM THAT STANDPOINT, YOU DON'T MEASURE UP.
THINGS ARE ALREADY PROBLEMATIC. SEGUCHI SHOWED ZERO INTEREST IN YOUR MUSIC WHEN YOU OPENED FOR ASK.
I'M STRIKING OUT ON MY OWN TO SCOUT YOU, WHICH MEANS I'M SECOND-GUESSING HIS INSTINCTS.
FOR ME, THE CORE POTENTIAL OF BAD LUCK IS SHINDOU'S SINGING AND HIRO'S GUITAR PLAYING.
OTHERWISE, I THINK SEGUCHI WAS RIGHT TO IGNORE YOU.

Well... HOW SHOULD I PUT THIS...
I THINK THAT WITH HARD WORK YOU CAN IMPROVE...
IN OTHER WORDS ...
YOU THINK I'M A TERRIBLE WRITER AND KEYBOARD PLAYER.
......
...BUT YOU'RE STILL A DIAMOND IN THE ROUGH. CONSIDER, THOUGH, THAT I'M NOT SUGGESTING YOU CHANGE YOUR STYLE.
I'D JUST RATHER PAIR YOU UP WITH A TOP-NOTCH SYNTH PLAYER.
I LIKE YOUR COMPUTER-GENERATED APPROACH. IT'S COLD AND MODERN.
I WANT TO SHAPE THAT TO BE HIT-WORTHY, AND I WANT TO MAKE YOU A SUPERSTAR FRONTMAN.

ULTIMATELY, I THINK YOU'LL SEE THIS AS WIN-WIN.
MMMMMM~~~
THAT PRICK!!
AAAGHH!
STOP SQUIRMING, SHUICHI! I'M GONNA KICK YOU OFF!
ぶんぶん
SUZUKI
Hiro's brother's bike...
YOUR BACK FEELS STRONG AND WARM...
Okay, okay...
LET'S RIDE LIKE THE WIND. ♡
↑ my foot!

I UNDERSTAND HOW YOU FEEL, DON'T GET ME WRONG.
I JUST THINK MAYBE YOU OVERREACTED.
You sure do eat a lot for a little guy...
Hmph?
munch
IT WAS PRETTY PAINFUL WATCHING YOU AND SAKANO GO AT IT...
Y'know?
You're saying I don't have talent?! You liar! What do you know?!
I-I'm sorry... That's not what I meant. It's not that you don't have talent... I'm sorry! I'm sorry!
You better listen to my demo tape again!
How can you not recognize my brilliance?! Something's wrong here! But it's not me. It's you!
Help, Seguchiiiiiii!
BUT...
Grab
HE SAID HE WAS GOING TO DO HIS BEST TO PROTECT OUR INTERESTS.
DIDN'T SOUND LIKE IT TO ME!
HOW CAN ANYONE BESIDES ME PLAY THE SYNTHESIZER FOR BAD LUCK?
Bad Luck = their band name

Pat
WELL, THERE'S NOTHING YOU CAN DO ABOUT THIS.

HM? ARE YOU SAYING THAT NO ONE CAN PLAY QUITE AS POORLY AS YOU?
Uh...
SCREW YOU! THAT'S NOT WHAT I MEANT. I'M A BRILLIANT KEYBOARD PLAYER!

YOU'RE JUST GOING TO HAVE TO ACCEPT IT AND MOVE ON. IT'S NOT ALL ABOUT US ANYMORE.
SOMETIMES YOU HAVE TO SACRIFICE FOR SUCCESS.
THIS IS WHAT IT MEANS TO BE PROFESSIONALS.

DO YOU HAVE TO BE SO FLIPPANT ABOUT IT?
TO ME IT DOESN'T MATTER WHETHER YOU'RE PLAYING THE SYNTHESIZER OR NOT...

...AS LONG AS I GET TO PLAY MUSIC WITH YOU...
...I'LL HAVE EVERYTHING I WANT.
You're making me blush.
BUT...
WHAT IF THE NEW SYNTH GUY IS A REAL GENIUS?
C'mon, get on!
No way!
What?
SUZUKI
THERE'S NO WAY ANYONE CAN BE BETTER...
Well, no one but Seguchi-san...
THE WORLD IS MINE!
THE KING
...THAN ME!!!
I'M NEVER RIDING WITH YOU AGAIN.
I'm starting the engine now.
SUZUKI
YOUR HAIR SMELLS NICE.
GET OFF, FREAK.
Sniff Sniff

ABOUT GRAVITATION TRACK 7, PART 2:

Hiro's dialogue explains it all, but their band Bad Luck mixes several genres—instrumentals, rap, techno, and hardcore dance. They also sing and do comedy routines. Whatever works. Who knows what they really are. Maybe it's kind of a guerilla style, attacking all kinds of music. Watch for these guys. Big dreams are worth dreaming, especially if they start to come true.

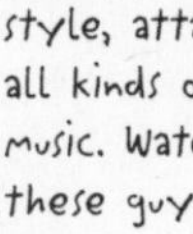

VROOO

ON THE BRIGHT SIDE... WE ALL AGREE YOUR SINGING IS REALLY AMAZING.

Huh? REALLY?

SURE. YOU HAVE A GREAT VOICE.

Hiro's back

VROOOOOM

I DIDN'T REALLY NOTICE IT BEFORE, SINCE WE'VE BEEN DOING SO MANY INSTRUMENTALS AND YOU'VE BEEN RAPPING A LOT.

I'M NOT SURE HOW TO DESCRIBE IT. IT'S LIKE IAN CURTIS. A MASSIVE, CRASHING WAVE OF SOUND.

Don't forget to look both ways!

What's that supposed to mean?

REALLY? I'M JUST SINGING, THAT'S ALL.

AIEEE

Warn me before you take off! You're gonna get me killed!

Drop dead!

VROOOM

YOU? A STAR?
SOUNDS TO ME LIKE THE END OF QUALITY JAPANESE MUSIC AS WE KNOW IT.
I GUESS SEGUCHI'S FINALLY GONE SENILE. HE USED TO BE SO HIP, TOO.
Stab
Stab
SINCE WHEN HAS N-G SIGNED COMEDY ACTS?
Stab
Stab
DON'T GET ALL POUTY, EITHER. YOU KNOW I'M GOING TO PICK ON YOU, SO WHY KEEP COMING AROUND?
DAMMIT!
I keep hoping you'll be nice for once!!
THAT'S YOU. ALWAYS THE DREAMER.
TO BE HONEST, I THINK YOU SHOULD BE HAPPY ABOUT THIS DEAL.
A little sensitive, aren't you?
YOU'RE SUCH A SOURPUSS.

Ha Ha Ha Ha
HAPPY!♡
I'M NUMBER ONE
Ha
THAT'S EXCESSIVE...
I said be happy, not act like an idiot.
On top of the table
NITTLE GRASPER
HEY...
WHOAAA!!
Now what?!
NITTLE GRASPER'S LIVE IN CONCERT VIDEO!!
AND IT'S THE LIMITED EDITION BUDOKAN FINAL PERFORMANCE!!
NITTLE GRASPER
WHAT ARE YOU DOING WITH THIS?!
-OH.
IT'S MY BROTHER'S. NOT MINE.
I'VE BEEN LOOKING EVERYWHERE FOR THIS VIDEO!
IT'S IMPOSSIBLE TO FIND!
YOUR BROTHER HAD IT?! WHAT LUCK!!
Tears of Gratitude

GO AHEAD, WATCH IT...
Loser.
AH!
The video remote!
Badum Badum Badum
Gulp!
THIS IS IT!! THE PASSION I'VE BEEN SEARCHING FOR THROUGHOUT MY EIGHTEEN YEARS ON EARTH!!
AAAAGHHHHH!
It's blinding!!
tears of joy
GOOD FOR YOU...
Fuu
NITTLE-GRASPE
Vocals:
RYUICHI SAKU
Keyboards:
TOHMA SEGUC
keyboards and vo
NORIKO UKAI
WHOAAAA
LOOK, LOOK! IT'S MY HERO!
RYUICHI SAKUMA! HE'S THE GUY WHO CHANGED MY LIFE!
forced to watch
GYAAAA! HE'S SO COOL! ISN'T HE COOL?!
SEE?! I'M YOUR BIGGEST FAN, SAKUMA-SAN!
I THOUGHT YOU WERE SEGUCHI'S BIGGEST FAN. ISN'T THAT WHY YOU STARTED PLAYING THE SYNTH?
YOU'RE PISSED AT HIM 'CAUSE HE DIDN'T LIKE YOUR TAPE?
TV

NO, THAT'S NOT IT.
TO ME, SEGUCHI-SAN IS SOMEONE I ASPIRED TO BE...
IT WAS BEYOND BEING A FAN. I WANTED TO BE LIKE HIM...
LET ME TELL YOU, SEGUCHI MAY SEEM LIKE A NICE GUY, BUT HE'S A SHARK.
THAT'S NOT TRUE! HE'S A GOOD PERSON!
きっ
A GOOD PERSON?
hmph
IF YOU BELIEVE THAT AND ASPIRE TO BE LIKE HIM...
むっ
...THEN YOU'RE FAILING MISERABLY, AREN'T YOU?

WHO THE HELL'S SEGUCHI?

ANGER

Who you callin' a failure?

JEEZ, YOU'RE A SPAZ...

Go home already!

YOU'RE BORING WHEN YOU'RE NOT ACTING STUPID...

BUT YOU'RE EVEN WORSE WHEN YOU'RE TRYING TOO HARD.

I AM NOT!

AND WHAT THE HELL DO YOU MEAN BY BORING ANYWAY?!

WHAT DO YOU DO THAT'S SO EXCITING?

pinch

IF YOU WANT TO GET ALL EMOTIONAL, THEN GO SOMEPLACE ELSE.

TAKE SOME RITALIN. I DON'T WANT TO HEAR YOU BITCH AND MOAN.

DON'T BE SUCH A WHINER. IT MAKES ME SICK.
I...
...I'M SORRY!
THAT'S NOT WHY I CAME HERE, EIRI, REALLY...
I'LL BE QUIET...
SO...
HEY!
!! YES?!

Squeeze
QUIT BEING SO NERVOUS ALL THE TIME.
Ahhh, I'm such a lucky guy... Yuki kissed me...
Well...
I'M NOT ANYMORE...
NOT JUST THAT, YOU IDIOT.
I MEAN, WHY SHOULD WE STOP THERE?
Huh?
Grip
I'M SURE YOU GET FRUSTRATED WITH JUST KISSING AND NEED A RELEASE.

WHA...?
I'M TOTALLY SATISFIED WITH JUST KISSING...!
GYAAAAA!
Help!
DON'T LIE.
I KNOW YOU HAVE A LOT OF PENT-UP LOVE.
That hurts!
NO... THAT'S NOT WHAT I WANT...
YOU'RE HEAVY...
SHUT UP.
Of course, he doesn't stand a chance...
You're scaring me!!
HEY !!
W-W-WAIT A MINUTE!!
ALL RIGHT, ALL RIGHT! I'LL DO IT!
I GIVE IN! JUST GIVE ME A SEC'!!

WHY IS THIS HAPPENING ??!
Don't give me that spooky look!
Stare
Badum Badum
UH... UH...
LOOK... YOU... I... WE...
I mean, you know...
WHAT AM I SAYING ?!
Tremble Tremble
IF YOU'RE GONNA DO THIS, YOU BETTER MEAN IT.
URK.
I'M TALKING LIKE A GIRL ABOUT TO GIVE UP HER VIRGINITY!!
I mean... It's practically the same thing.
FINE.
Sure thing.
I'LL BE YOUR LOVER FROM NOW ON.

BUT THAT MEANS...

I GET TO GO ALL THE WAY, SHUICHI.

WHAT? WAIT A MINUTE...

Uh, hello?

YOU DON'T GET TO CRY UNCLE IN THE MIDDLE LIKE THE LAST TIME THINGS GOT A LITTLE SWEATY, OKAY?

You serious?

HANG ON!
WHY ARE YOU ACTING LIKE YOU LIKE ME ALL OF A SUDDEN?!
I THOUGHT YOU SAID I WAS SOME KIND OF PERVERT?!
EEEEEEK!
Thunk!
YOU TALK TOO DAMN MUCH.
YOU WANT TO HAVE A CONVERSATION, OR DO YOU WANT TO BE MY LOVER?
OWWW
IT'S ABOUT TIME YOU GOT HONEST.
YOUR COWARDICE IS IRRITATING.

WHAT I REALLY WANT IS...

HM?
...I WANTED TO BE JUST LIKE HIM.
Help me, somebody help me...
Oh, Sakuma-san, you're so cool...
I've come to a treacherous border...
I know it's time to say good-bye......
I CAN'T EVEN GET CLOSE TO TOUCHING YOUR TALENT.
CAN I...?
But can you help me restore order...
Before we let our love die.

YES...
I CAN BE BETTER THAN HIM. I FEEL IT. ONE DAY...
HEY, THAT CHICK NEXT TO HIM HAS A SMOKIN' BODY.
ARE YOU EVEN LISTENING ...?
WHEN ALL OF OUR BUSINESS IS TAKEN CARE OF, I'LL LISTEN TO YOU YAP ALL YOU WANT.
ぐい
HEY!
YO, WAIT...
SHOVE!

OWW!
THAT HURTS!
Yuki!
OH, SHIT, HE'S REALLY SERIOUS!
Calm and Collected
IT HURTS, DAMMIT...
You're too strong!
YOU BETTER NOT LEAVE ME...
EIRI ...
CAN'T YOU BE MORE GENTLE...?
Owww!
SHUT UP.
Ahh!
Ahh!
Ahh!
YOU'D BETTER BE MY BOYFRIEND!!
twinge
Ahh!

HM?
You're quick.
heh
SHUT UP!!
I'm young and inexperienced, okay?!
OH, YEAH? OKAY, OKAY.
ぬぎ
OR MAYBE I'M JUST THAT GOOD.
READY FOR THE NEXT LEVEL?
NO WAY!
YOU MEAN WE REALLY HAVE TO DO IT?!
OF COURSE. YOU CAN'T HAVE ALL THE FUN.
B-b-but but but...
DON'T WORRY.
Y-
YUKI...
I'm scared...
Sob
Sob
Sob

Sob Sob Sob Sob Sob Sob Sob Sob Sob Sob

I'M TRYING MY BEST TO BE REALLY NICE TO YOU.

Don't you think you're being rude?

I'M BEING RAPED HERE!! IT'S A BIT NEW TO ME!

HOW CAN I NOT BE SCARED?!

Raped?!

BUT YOU JUST SAID...

...THAT YOU WANTED MY LOVE.

No...

NO...

WHAT I WANT IS...

YOU WANT THIS, RIGHT?

NO! NO!

SEX...SEX ISN'T WHAT I'M AFTER...
THEN WHAT?
WHAT IS IT?
...?
I'M PUTTING IT ON THE LINE FOR YOU...
YUKI...
...SO, DON'T SAY SOMETHING STUPID.
Idiot!
Jerk!

OWWWWWWWW!!
到着ロビー
Arrival Lobby
団体受付
Group Check-in
SEGUCHI! SIR!
lunch
YOU MUST BE TIRED AFTER YOUR LONG FLIGHT FROM NEW YORK.
MMPH MMMMPH MMPHHHH.
Seguchi ...
He's in the same rhythm!
Just to let you know, Sakano's been struck by a sudden, unexplainable maternal instinct.
mmphh

LONG TIME NO SEE.
HOW HAVE YOU BEEN?
YOU'RE ALWAYS A WELCOME SIGHT, NORIKO.
OH, COME ON! YOU DON'T SHOW A SINGLE DAY OF YOUR THIRTY YEARS, TOHMA!
You freak of nature!
THAT'S ONE HELL OF A WAY TO GREET ME AFTER THREE YEARS APART.
I'M SURE WE'LL HAVE PLENTY OF TIME TO CATCH UP LATER.
JAL
Group Check-in
OUR CAR IS WAITING. SHALL WE GO?

N-G IS A PRETTY BIG LABEL. I CAN'T BELIEVE YOU'RE THE PRESIDENT.
I'D SAY THAT EASILY MAKES YOU THE MOST SUCCESSFUL EX-GRASPER, TOHMA.
stab
UNDERLING
LOOKS LIKE YOU HAVE PRETTY GOOD TASTE IN UNDERLINGS, TOO!
OH, CHILL OUT. I'M JUST KIDDING!
Don't get all bummed!
So sad...
IF YOU WANT TO BE A BIG LEAGUE PRODUCER, ACT LIKE IT!
YOU CAN'T LET SOME EIGHTEEN-YEAR-OLD PIZZA-FACED KID PUSH YOU AROUND!
IF YOU HAVE TO KICK HIS ASS, THEN DO IT! KICK HIS ASS!
She's been like this ever since we got here, Seguchi.
Sorry. Noriko's been that way since forever...
IT'S YOUR JOB TO KEEP THE ROOKIES IN LINE LONG ENOUGH FOR THEM TO BECOME STARS.

YOU'RE RIGHT.
BUT MAYBE WHAT SHUICHI REALLY NEEDS IS A WOMAN'S TOUCH, EH, NORIKO?
ふふん
MAYBE.
BUT I DOUBT IT.
BESIDES, SAKANO IS GOING TO HAVE TO MAKE SHUICHI LISTEN IF HE WANTS HIS RESPECT.
THAT KID WILL SEE THE LIGHT, ONCE HE REALIZES HIS PRODUCER MAKES ALL THE RIGHT CHOICES...
SOMETHING YOU AND I KNOW ABOUT SAKANO ALREADY, RIGHT, TOHMA?

IT'S A TESTAMENT TO YOUR GENIUS THAT YOU CALLED ME YOUR NUMBER ONE PUPIL, EH, SEGUCHI?

BECAUSE I'VE GOT IT ALL FIGURED OUT.

IT'S BEEN THREE YEARS SINCE WE BROKE UP THE BAND.

I CAN REMEMBER HIM SINGING UP ON STAGE LIKE IT WAS YESTERDAY.

I SHOULD HAVE SEEN IT ON MY OWN.
THE PUPIL TEACHES THE TEACHER. I GUESS I'M GETTING OLD, AREN'T I, SAKANO?
Huh?
oh no
Actually, he's younger!
WELL, LET THE POWER OF YOUTH PREVAIL.
MAKE ME EAT MY WORDS.
SHOW ME THAT HARD WORK CAN OVERCOME ANY DEFICIT OF TALENT.
I'LL BE LOOKING FORWARD TO YOUR RESULTS, SAKANO.
OR SHOULD I SAY, PRODUCER.
Uh, yes?

HEY!

HOW LONG ARE YOU GONNA JUST LIE THERE?

IT'S USUALLY THE PITCHER WHO GETS TIRED DURING THE GAME.

YOU'RE AN ANIMAL!

It hurts, owwwww...

I feel sick, ughh!

I wanna go to the bathroom...

...but I can't get up.

YOU CAN'T LET ME REST FOR A SECOND, CAN YOU?!

JEEZ, WE ONLY DID IT THREE TIMES.
Come on, you're still young.
THREE IS A LOT!

I KNOW YOU WERE WHINING ABOUT IT HURTING AT FIRST...

...BUT YOU NEVER TOLD ME TO STOP.

AND IF I PICK ON YOU, YOU CRY EVEN MORE.

EVEN WHEN I VISITED MY DAD FOR YOU, OR YOU ASKED ME TO MAKE LOVE TO YOU, OR TO KISS YOU...

...NO MATTER WHAT I DO, YOU'RE NEVER HAPPY.

SO, FINALLY, I MAKE LOVE TO YOU...
I TELL YOU I'LL MAKE YOU MY LOVER.
WHAT ELSE CAN I POSSIBLY DO?
HOW CAN I MAKE YOU HAPPY?
ぎゅ
YUKI...
YUKI... I...

にたあ

← drool

I'M HAPPY

GYAAAAAA!

WHAT ARE YOU DOING?! YOU TOLD ME TO SMILE, SO I DID!

SHUT UP, YOU WORM. GET OUT, AND DON'T EVER COME BACK!

Here!

YOU SAID YOU WANTED ME TO BE YOUR LOVER! HOW CAN YOU BE SO COLD?!

WHAT ARE YOU TALKING ABOUT? WHEN DID I SAY THAT?

I'm getting rid of this anyway!

WHY YOU...!!

The dresser

worried
N-
LOUNGE
ADB
I SEE...
SO SHINDOU HAS AGREED TO CONCENTRATE EXCLUSIVELY ON HIS VOCALS FOR THE TIME BEING.

I CUT MY TRIP TO NEW YORK SHORT BECAUSE I WANTED HER TO PLAY WITH BAD LUCK. IT TOOK SOME CONVINCING...

SO PLEASE, GIVE HER A FAIR SHAKE.

HER?

Clack!
HEY...
YOU'RE LATE, SAKANO...
ばん
HEY THERE!
IT'S PICO-PICO NORIKO-CHAN! YOU GUYS BEEN WAITING LONG?
!!!
track7 ▶ END

TOHMA
SEGUCHI

NITTLE GRASPER.

THE GROUP DISBANDED THREE YEARS AGO.
VOCALS: RYUICHI SAKUMA
KEYBOARDS: TOHMA SEGUCHI
AND ME: NORIKO UKAI.

NOWADAYS, RYU HAS EMBARKED ON A SOLO CAREER, AND TOHMA IS A PRODUCER.

I'M WORKING AS A STUDIO MUSICIAN SUPPORTING A NEWBIE BAND.

ALTHOUGH, THIS NEW KID BEARS SOME RESEMBLANCE TO A CERTAIN VOCALIST FROM MY PAST LIFE...

THAT'S AWFUL! WHAT'S WRONG WITH YOUR VOICE?! IT SOUNDS LIKE YOU'RE GARGLING A CAT'S NUT SACK!

THE SONG IS AWESOME!! YOU SHOULD KISS MY FEET IN GRATITUDE, NOT PISS ALL OVER IT! DO IT AGAIN!!

STUDIO B

U-UKAI... YOU DON'T NEED TO BE SO HARSH.

PRODUCER

SUPPORT MEMBER

ARE YOU LISTENING TO ME, YOU LITTLE SHIT?! SPEAK UP! WHAT DO YOU HAVE TO SAY FOR YOURSELF?

ABOUT GRAVITATION TRACK 8

I'd like to talk a little about Nittle Grasper. My relationship with them goes back a long way. I actually first created them a little over three years ago. Not on paper, but in my head. A cheerful and playful vocalist; a loving, angelic synth player; and a tomboyish-but-cute girl as a second keyboard player. Your basic electronic trio. The blueprint for these characters became the basis for all of my manga. Pretty simple, right? I guess I need a new trick. (kaboom)

UGGGHHH
Gimme a break...
DO I HAVE TO START ALL OVER?! THIS IS THE 20TH TIME, NORIKO! THAT'S WHY MY VOICE IS SHOT!
OKAY!
YOU HEARD ME. FROM THE TOP! AND THIS TIME GIVE IT SOME FUN AND ENERGY!
ほ
LOVE, WITH
Energetic and fun...
WITH YOU...
UGH, MY THROAT!
I THINK THAT MELODY IS GOING TO HAUNT ME IN MY SLEEP.
moan
Okay, Hiro, that's perfect!
I'M SORRY. UKAI IS PRETTY DEMANDING, BUT THAT'S WHY SHE'S THE BEST.

SHE ONLY GETS SO WORKED UP BECAUSE SHE HAS SUCH BIG HOPES FOR YOU.

YOU REMIND HER OF GRASPER'S VOCALIST.

WHA—?

YOU MEAN SAKUMA?! ME?!

WHAAAAAT?!

MORON?!
YOU MEAN I'M JUST AS STUPID AS SAKUMA?! YIPPEE! I ♡ MADE IT! ♡ ♡
I'm so lucky!
Whoa, calm down!
uh...
I FEEL SORRY FOR SAKUMA BEING COMPARED TO HIM...
I'M GOING TO BE TAKING OFF.
Good job!
ばたばた
WAIT! HIRO! LET'S GO HOME TOGETHER!
WHAT ARE YOU? A LITTLE KID?
WHAT'S THE MATTER? CAN'T I GO HOME WITH YOU?

YOU'RE SO CRUEL, HIRO... I THOUGHT WE WERE PALS...
WAAAAAH!
CAN'T WE GO HOME TOGETHER? P-P-PLEASE?
ALL RIGHT ALREADY. LET'S GET OUT OF HERE.
DON'T TELL ME YOU'VE BEEN LIVING ON YOUR OWN FOR TWO DAYS AND YOU'RE HOMESICK ALREADY?!
T-THAT'S NOT IT!
BESIDES...
AS YOUR BEST FRIEND, IT'S PROBABLY GOOD THAT WE MEET.
WHO MEET?
EIRI YUKI. THAT'S WHERE YOU'RE GOING, RIGHT?

WHAT?
HOW DID YOU...?
I HAD A HUNCH.

JUDGING BY YOUR REACTION, THAT HUNCH WAS RIGHT.
AH HA HA HA HA HA!

SEE YA TOMORROW MORNING!
DUDE, YOU DON'T HAVE TO BE SO BASHFUL.

IT'S OKAY.
LET ME MEET HIM. I'LL BE GOOD.
OKAY...
BUT YOU DON'T GET TO TOUCH HIM.

ABOUT GRAVITATION TRACK 8, PART 2:

The Lolita-ization of Shuichi continues. Do you readers remember our first sidebar for Track 1 in Book 1? Even then Shuichi's rambunctiousness was above normal levels. In addition to saying that he can be a real airhead, I mentioned that I'd like to see him continue to be a pretty straightforward guy. But I underestimated him. Straight and narrow? He's shot up like the Tower of Babel! And now he's become such a baby! Something like this.

I wonder what it is. I get mail from my readers commenting that they enjoy seeing Shuichi because he's cute, but can't I make him a little cooler? I don't know if they're just taking jabs at me or what. Anyway, sorry for all the confusion.

WHAT HE LACKS IN SINGING ABILITY, HE MAKES UP FOR IN CHARISMA.
THE KID HAS THE SPARK.
I THINK HE'D IMPROVE EVEN IF LEFT TO HIS OWN DEVICES.
I'M SURE HE'D BE HONORED TO RECEIVE SUCH HIGH PRAISE FROM A FORMER GRASPER.
THANK YOU.

DIGGING UP THE PAST IS A PATHETIC EXERCISE.
IT ONLY SERVES TO REMIND US WE'RE GETTING OLDER.
Oh, woe is me, somebody turn back time! Like Cher!
sob
badum badum badum
OH, NOW YOU'RE BEING SILLY.
You don't look old at all. Honest.
I'm just kidding!
WE'LL PUT DOWN A FEW TRACKS OVER THE NEXT COUPLE OF DAYS.
AND THE SINGLE IS COMING OUT ON THE TENTH OF NEXT MONTH, RIGHT?
ARE YOU PLANNING ANY LIVE PERFORMANCES TO TIE IN WITH THE RELEASE?
WELL...
smile
THEY'VE PLAYED AT ALL THE BEST CLUBS AROUND TOWN AS OPENING ACTS FOR OTHER BANDS...
...SO I FIGURED WE'D HIT THE SAME VENUES AS HEADLINERS.
UGHH!
I KNEW IT!
IT'S SO PREDICTABLE!

ARE YOU ALWAYS THIS DULL? DO YOU EVEN KNOW THE WORD "AMBITION"?
IF YOU WANT BAD LUCK TO LEAVE ASK AT THE BOTTOM OF THE CHARTS, YOU'VE GOT TO THINK BIGGER THAN THAT!
どき
ビク
BUT...I'VE ALREADY BOOKED THE TOUR...
OH, COME ON! YOU'RE YOUNGER THAN ME...
BUT YOU'RE THINKING LIKE AN OLD MAN! CAN'T YOU BE MORE CREATIVE?!
I-I'm sorry...
Quit being such a jellyfish, man!
WE NEED TO DO SOMETHING MASSIVE! YOU'VE GOT TO HAVE LIGHTS AND PYROTECHNICS, AND HAVE SOME HUGE, FAMOUS GUEST STAR DROP BY TO JAM WITH THE BOYS!
WELL, IF YOU'RE SO SMART, DO YOU HAVE ANY IDEAS?
OF COURSE.
WHAT DO YOU THINK I JUST SAID?

BUT THEN, I'M JUST A HIRED GUN IN THIS BAND.
IT'S JUST A SUGGESTION.
BUT IF I GET A THUMBS UP...
FROM BAD LUCK'S PRODUCER, THEN JUST ABOUT ANYTHING'S POSSIBLE, ISN'T IT, KIDDO?
...

IS THIS WHERE YUKI LIVES?
YEAH. IT'S JUST A LEFT AT THE CORNER, THEN RIGHT.
YOUR NEW APARTMENT'S IN THIS NEIGHBORHOOD, TOO, ISN'T IT?
UH, YEAH, HA HA...
NOW I KNOW WHY YOU CHOSE TO SHACK UP HERE.
Dude, you're creepy.
NO, IT'S JUST CHEAP...
PLEASE, LET ME GO!
OH, COME ON. JUST A LITTLE BIT...
y'know?

DON'T BE SUCH A SQUARE. WE JUST WANNA SING SOME KARAOKE.
Long hair
IT'S NOT FUN WHEN IT'S JUST US.
I-I JUST WANTED TO ASK DIRECTIONS ...
Ooh, classic scenario!
WELL, WELL. IT APPEARS A COUPLE OF RUFFIANS ARE PESTERING AN INNOCENT GIRL.
I'M SORRY, HIRO. I DON'T KNOW ANY SHORT CUTS TO GET PAST HERE.
INTER-ESTING.
HEY!
WHAT?!

Shindou! I love NY!

WHAT--?!
YOU SCUM-BAGS...
I DON'T JUST GIVE ANYONE MY AUTOGRAPH!
Who said we wanted one?
BOYS WHO CAN'T SAY "THANK YOU" OR "I'M SORRY" CAN NEVER MAKE FRIENDS...
AND END UP DATING THEIR HANDS.
Since when did you get so tough?
DUDE, THAT'S HARD-CORE.
Sound of the pen hitting the ground

SORRY ABOUT THAT... MISS, ARE YOU ALL RIGHT?
YOU'RE NOT HURT...? HM?
Hey, how about a "thank you"?!
Th-thank you!
Gyaaaaa!!
Okay, now your buddy can have an autograph...
No, please, don't!
HEY, SHUICHI!
LET'S GO EAT.

OH, DO YOU GUYS WANNA GO EAT TOO?

HELL NO!

I hate you bastards!

Help, Mommy!

UH...
THANK YOU FOR RESCUING ME. IF YOU HADN'T...
ツテリア
WHAT'S A YOUNG HIGH SCHOOL GIRL LIKE YOU DOING OUT AT 1:00 IN THE MORNING?
Really!
DID YOU RUN AWAY FROM HOME?
munch もぐ もぐ munch
IT'S NOT THAT...
THERE WAS SOMEONE I HAD TO MEET...
I CAME HERE SPECIFICALLY TO FIND HIM.

SO YOU WERE LOOKING FOR SOMEONE.
I SEE. INTER-ESTING ...
That's a mighty mission...!
I...
I'M SORRY. I DON'T MEAN TO BORE YOU WITH MY PERSONAL PROBLEMS.

SO...
WHAT'S YOUR NAME?
Uh...
OH!
MY NAME IS AYAKA.

HELLO, AYAKA.
NICE TO MEET YOU. WOULD YOU LIKE US TO ESCORT YOU BACK HOME?

BUT... I LIVE IN KYOTO...

Like going home with these guys is any less scary!

THEN WHY DON'T YOU STAY AT MY PLACE FOR A COUPLE OF DAYS.
...
Uh... well...
IT'S A LONG WAY TO KYOTO.
I'M SURE YOUR PARENTS MUST BE WORRIED...
I WAS RIGHT... SHE RAN AWAY!
AND WHAT ABOUT SCHOOL?
sob
I...
I HAVE TO MEET SOMEONE...
AND UNTIL I DO, I CAN'T LEAVE...
BOO HOO HOO

OKAY, IT'S SETTLED. IN ORDER TO FULFILL HER MISSION, AYAKA WILL BE USING MY PLACE AS A COMMAND CENTER.
WHAT KIND OF LOGIC IS THAT?
I'M GOING HOME.
I'D TAKE HER TO THE POLICE IF I WERE YOU, HIRO!
Sure thing...
AND DON'T YOU WORK TOO HARD TONIGHT, SHINDOU. SAVE A LITTLE OF YOUR THROAT FOR SINGING!
SHUT UP!
DJ AT WOR
MAYBE SHE'S HERE TO SEE HER BOYFRIEND ...
SHE LOOKS LIKE SHE PROBABLY COMES FROM A GOOD FAMILY. MAYBE HER BOYFRIEND IS FROM THE WRONG SIDE OF THE TRACKS AND HER PARENTS ARE AGAINST HER DATING HIM...

THANK GOODNESS.
HIS LIGHTS ARE STILL ON.
la la
I made it!
BZZZZ
brush brush
fixing his hair
しーん
NO ANSWER...

a rock
HEY, ARE YOU ASLEEP ?!
C'mon, dammit!
"SHUT THE HELL UP! I'M COMING!!"
IT'S YUKI'S VOICE!
PHEROMONE EXPLOSION! ENDORPHINS! ECSTASY!!!
ahhh
eeeek
O-OKAY! TONIGHT I'M GONNA BE BRAVE AND GREET HIM WITH A JAUNTY "IT'S ME!"
(a personal journey)
badum
badum
badum
SON OF A BITCH!
WHY DON'T YOU HAVE A KEY?!
click
It's me...

....
BLACK HAIR?!
echo echo...

HEY, UH, YUKI...
Uh...
IT'S YOU UNDER THERE, RIGHT? WHAT'S UP WITH YOUR HAIR...?
Your eyes are black, too.
YUKI?
OH, YOU MEAN EIRI.
MY BIG BROTHER ISN'T HERE RIGHT NOW, SHUICHI.
UH...
YOU SURPRISED ME.
YOU LOOK JUST LIKE MY SISTER DESCRIBED. YOU ARE SHUICHI, RIGHT?
BROTHER ?!
THIS GUY IS YUKI'S LITTLE BROTHER?!

stretch
MY NAME IS TATSUHA.
TATSUHA UESUGI.
Hi there!
Strange name... like a monk's son...
HUH? YOU'RE YUKI'S BROTHER BUT YOU HAVE DIFFERENT LAST NAMES?
He never told me...
You idiot!
YUKI IS MY BROTHER'S PEN NAME. DIDN'T YOU KNOW THAT?
YOU'RE HIS LOVER AND YOU DON'T KNOW HIS NAME?
WHAT DO YOU THINK?
It's all rather confusing.
DON'T ASK ME!

ガバッ

ビクッ

Hey

HEYYYYYYY!!

DJ AT WORK

NO WAY!

ME TOO! TOTALLY! I'M A BIG FAN OF RYUICHI SAKUMA, TOO!! WE'RE SO ALIKE!

← his right hand

A Kindred Spirit

SAKUMA IS THE COOLEST EVER.
So, which Grasper song do you like the best? I like the 8th song in the Budokan set-"Be There." I like the lyrics. Or "Please Help Me." That one makes me horny as a high school band.
The encore to that show is phenomenal. Ryuichi takes off his shirt. And him and Seguchi are getting it on in front of everyone.
Hey, you sure know your music, Tatsuha-san.
Yeah?
Yeah, well, whatever.
So how did you get this video, Tatsuha? Did you get it from your sister?
Idiot, my sister isn't that generous. I had to go to a store and buy it.
video pamphlet card
HEY.
Y'know...
Kindred Spirit

YEAH? WHAT'S UP?

YOU LOOK LIKE RYUICHI.

EEK! YOU NOTICED? I COPIED HIS HAIR-STYLE. ♡
I EVEN USE THE SAME SHAMPOO. IT'S HERBAL!
See?
WELL, YEAH, THE HAIR...
BUT I WAS ALSO TALKING ABOUT YOUR BODY TYPE AND FACE.
REALLY?
YOU THINK SO? SHUT UP!
IT'S TRUE. IT'S IN THE SHOULDERS.
AND YOU'RE SMALL, BUT YOU'RE SKINNY LIKE HE IS.
Uh ...
ARE YOU REALLY A GUY?
ずぼ
Uh, well...
IF YOU'RE AS ALIKE AS I THINK...
...RYUICHI'S CHEST IS PROBABLY JUST LIKE YOURS, TOO.
sigh

I'M TOLD I LOOK LIKE MY BROTHER. DO YOU THINK SO?

HUH?

I'M GETTING...

...A BAD...

IT'S NOT JUST THE FACE.

I BET YOU I FUCK LIKE HIM, TOO.

CARE TO TEST THE THEORY?

!!!

...FEELING ABOUT THIS!!

NO, THAT'S OKAY!

WHILE WE DO IT, YOU CAN CALL ME EIRI, AND I'LL CALL YOU RYUICHI. WE'LL BOTH BE SOMEONE ELSE.

It'll be like virtual sex, y'know?

ARE YOU CRAZY?!

AAGHH!

KNOCK IT OFF! WE'RE BOTH DUDES!!

YOU MEAN HE'S BI?!

How many father figures can I have?

WELL, DUH.

IT'D BE ALL WRONG IF WE WEREN'T.

AAGHH!

guarding his privates

YOU MAY BE INTO DUDES, BUT I'M NOT!!!

Move that hand!

DON'T LIE. I KNOW YOU SLEEP WITH MY BROTHER.

YUKI'S DIFFERENT... HE'S SPECIAL...

HE'S...

SOMEBODY HELP...!

DON'T STOP.

PLEASE CONTINUE.

BREAKING AND ENTERING, STATUTORY RAPE.
YOU'RE SOME CRIMINAL, BRO.
You're heavy!
MY RAP SHEET IS NOTHING COMPARED TO THE LIST OF GIRLS YOU BANGED AND BAILED ON.
ONE OF THEM SENT THIS KEY.
HITOMI, I THINK HER NAME IS...?
Oh, really?
clink
FUNNY, BECAUSE HITOMI WANTED ME TO TELL YOU...
...SHE HAD FUN THE OTHER DAY AND IS HOPING YOU'LL TAKE HER OUT FOR A SHAG NEXT SATURDAY.
clump

IT'S HARD ENOUGH TO KEEP OUR CHICKS STRAIGHT, SINCE WE LIKE THEM THE SAME...
BUT IF WE'RE GONNA START SHARING THE FELLAS...
Is this all booze?
It sure ain't water.
I DON'T SEE A PROBLEM.
I'M NOT ATTRACTED TO OLDER MEN THE WAY YOU ARE.
DON'T MAKE FUN OF MY RYUICHI! HE'S ADORABLE!
......
YEAH, ADORABLY 30, YOU IMBECILE.
WOW! EVEN YOUR VOICES ARE ALIKE!
IT'S LIKE YUKI COMES IN TWO COLORS!
My neck is getting tired!
YOU GUYS COULD HAVE YOUR OWN SITCOM!

WHAT THE HELL ARE YOU TALKING ABOUT?
DID HAVING MY BROTHER INSIDE OF YOU INFECT YOU WITH STUPID?
YOU'RE GETTING ON MY NERVES. GO BURY YOURSELF.

WHOA. HE REALLY WENT AND BURIED HIMSELF.
'BOUT TIME.

Oh yeah!
I ALMOST FORGOT!
I BROUGHT US SOMETHING TO EAT WHILE WE DRINK.
I'm starving!

C-CAN I SIT NEXT TO YOU?
GO AHEAD.
hee
YUKI...
YOU AND YOUR BROTHER SEEM LIKE BEST PALS.
MAYBE.

HMPH.
MY SKIN IS PALE, AND MY EYES AND HAIR ARE LIGHT. I LOOK LIKE AN AMERICAN, DON'T I?
Hey, look, it's the Uesugi boy, Eiri. Doesn't he look mixed? Isn't that cute?
I GOT PICKED ON A LOT AS A KID, AND EVEN MY PARENTS LOOKED AT ME FUNNY.
MY BROTHER'S THE ONLY ONE WHO NEVER TREATED ME DIFFERENTLY.
HE'S ALWAYS BEEN THAT WAY.
Oh......
I THOUGHT YOU WERE MIXED, TOO.
IF THAT TURNS YOU ON, YOU CAN GO AHEAD AND THINK THAT.
NO! I DON'T!
FORGET IT...
His way of being kind.

SO HOW OLD ARE YOU? ARE YOU IN COLLEGE?

ME? I'M 16. AND I'M A MONK.

16?! A MONK ?!

YUP.

IF I PRAYED FOR HIM, EVEN THE DEVIL COULD MAKE IT TO HEAVEN.

HE'S TWO YEARS YOUNGER THAN ME, DAMMIT!!

IF YOU HAVE ANY FUNERALS COMING UP, SHUICHI, GIVE ME A CALL.

YEAH... IF YOU WANT TO CONDEMN THEIR SOUL.

munch

munch

munch

munch

...

YOU GOT THE MUNCHIES, EIRI? THAT'S YOUR FIFTH CAKE!

YOU CAUSE ME TO HAVE A BIG APPETITE.
I'm still hungry, too!
WHAT ARE YOU HERE FOR, ANYWAY, TATSUHA?
I'M LOOKING FOR SOMEONE.
I KNOW SHE'S SOMEWHERE AROUND HERE.
SEEN ANY ODDBALL DAMES?
took off his socks!
Yuki, please stop. That's your sixth one already! You'll die!
The sixth cake!

...
A LONG-HAIRED KYOTO BEAUTY...
munch
Oh, nooooo. Yuki, you'll turn into a butterball! You're out of control!
SHE'S THE ONLY DAUGHTER OF THE RYUGANJI TEMPLE FAMILY.
HER NAME IS AYAKA USAMI.
AYAKA?!
IT'S HER!!!

OH, GOOD MORNING, SHUICHI...
WHO'S THIS? HAVEN'T WE MET? AT TOHMA-KUN'S WEDDING, MAYBE?
THIS IS SEGUCHI'S WIFE'S BROTHER'S BROTHER!!
THAT'S NOT IMPORTANT, THOUGH. IS HIRO HERE?!
HELLO. IT'S BEEN A LONG TIME, EH? ♡
smile
ニコニコ
playing the part of a clean-cut youth → (it's in the genes!)

WOW. YOU'VE GROWN INTO A HANDSOME YOUNG MAN. ARE YOU INTO OLDER WOMEN?
DO YOU HAVE A GIRLFRIEND?
Yeah, I have about 15...
I'M ASKING IF HIRO'S HERE?!
Stop hitting on him!
HIRO'S RIGHT OVER...
OH, THERE HE IS.
I don't suppose Ryuichi is around.
GOOD MORNING.
I'm sleepy.
ガチャ
HIROOOOO!!!!
でこ
ぐおっ
お～っ
Whaaaaaa?!

DAMN YOU! WHERE WERE YOU LAST NIGHT! OUT PROWLING AROUND?!
badum badum
badum
I CALLED YOU 397 TIMES! YOU OWE ME AN EXPLANATION!
I didn't even get to sleep with Yuki last night!
I-I'M SORRY...

AYAKA AND MY BIG BROTHER AND I FORGOT ABOUT EVERYTHING AND WE WERE UP ALL NIGHT DOING KARAOKE.
Hiroshi, I'm gonna do Diana Ross, so you be the Supremes.
Alright.

THAT'S JUST IT! IT'S ABOUT AYAKA...

OH, HER? YEAH, SHE DOESN'T KNOW ANY CURRENT SONGS.
She's kind of odd. She thinks Interpol is just a detective agency. Can you imagine?!
THAT'S NOT THE POINT.

WHAT?!

REMEMBER SHE WAS SAYING SHE WANTED TO MEET WITH SOMEBODY?!

WELL, I FOUND THAT SOMEBODY! I EVEN BROUGHT HIM HERE!!

BLAH

ふんふんっ

huff はぁ huff はぁっ

ぱん

THAT'S GREAT!

ISN'T IT?!

AYAKA, DID YOU HEAR THAT?

HUH?

OH, YEAH... SHE SAID SHE WANTED TO SEE THE STUDIO, SO I BROUGHT HER ALONG.

Whoa, what luck!

thumbs up

I DON'T UNDERSTAND YOU, GIRL. IF YOU HAVE THE TIME TO MESS AROUND, WHY DON'T YOU JUST GO HOME?

You go out all night karaoking with some strange guy? Clearly finding Tatsuha wasn't all that important to your fickle ass.

TATSUHA !!
WHAT ARE YOU DOING HERE...?
I FINALLY FOUND YOU, MY PRINCESS.
I'M SURE YOUR PARENTS MUST BE HAVING A HISSY FIT.
TATSU-HA...
What's going on?
Dunno...
NO! I DON'T WANT TO GO HOME! I HAVE TO SEE HIM!!

HUH?
HEY!
YO, TATSUHA!!
ISN'T AYAKA YOUR FORBIDDEN GIRLFRIEND?!
HUH? WELL...
hmph
PLENTY TOUGH
twitch
UGH...
WHY WON'T HE SEE ME?!
UWAAAAH!
I HATE YOU, EIRI!!
PLENTY TOUGH

I DON'T CARE IF YOU'RE IN LOVE WITH SOMEONE ELSE. I'M DIFFERENT!
WHAT?
I CAN MAKE YOU FORGET ANYONE...!!
PLENTY TOUGH
THERE'S NO WAY...

NOW, LOOK, SHUICHI...
Oh, man...
I WAS TRYING TO KEEP MY MOUTH SHUT BECAUSE I DIDN'T WANT YOU TO KNOW, BUT...
THIS GIRL ISN'T MY GIRLFRIEND ...
I'M EIRI'S...
I'M EIRI'S FIANCÉE!!
EIRI IS ENGAGED ...TO THIS GIRL?!
track8▶END

favorite food:
strawberry pocky

SHUICHI SHINDOU

Favorite food:
strawberry shortcake

EIRI YUKI

The following is my very first published work. I present it to you with a mixture of joy, fear, and embarrassment. Personally, I like it very much, but I don't know how you guys will react. When I think about how abnormal my tastes have gotten since my debut, I have to laugh...

All the characters' names are based on people I know. And the title was something thought up by one of my editors. Anyway, given its significance in the start of my career, it's still close to my heart. It also established a method of working that I still use today.

The Tragedy of the Narcissist

2-10
MY NAME IS TATSUYA UESUGI. A SHINING SYMBOL OF YOUTH AT 17.
ガラッ
GOOD MORNING, EVERYBODY!
Yo, shut up, fool, and then y'know. Ha ha ha
LOVE ME
FOR STARTERS, I'M POPULAR WITH THE LADIES.
EEEEE!
GOOD MORNING, UESUGI!
GOOD MORNING, HONEY! YOU'RE LOOKING HANDSOME!
Oh my god, really?!
très bien!
I made a lunch for you.
Thank you!
I GET ABOUT 20,000 LETTERS IN MY MAILBOX EVERY DAY.
I'll let you cheat off me on the next test.
Thank you.
YOU COULD SAY I RULE THE WORLD...
......
eee!
eeeee!
......

...BECAUSE I'M
BEAUTIFUL!!
Heyyyyy...
TATSUYA!
LET'S EAT LUNCH TOGETHER.
pfffft
WITH YOU? FORGET IT.
You'll infect me with ugly.
...
JUST KIDDING. DUMMY.
CLOSED
DO NOT DISTURB
S-SO WE CLOSED OFF THE LIBRARY TO EAT...?
I don't know if I should be impressed or appalled...
Here we go.
IF WE EAT IN THE CLASSROOM, THE GIRLS ARE JUST GONNA DISTURB US.
HUH, YOU'RE ONLY EATING BREAD? NO BENTO TODAY?
Didn't the girls make you lunch?
THAT'S THAT!
I ONLY EAT MEALS PREPARED BY BEAUTIFUL GIRLS.
I see...

*Original List: Kumiko Goto, Yuki Uchida, Arisa Mizuki, Shinji Takada, and Ai Iijima.

HEY, YOU ALL RIGHT?
OWWWWW!
WHY YOU ...
WATCH WHERE YOU'RE GOING, YOU IDIOT!
WHAT IF YOU HIT MY PRECIOUS FACE?!
WHAT ?!
huh ?
SHUT THE HELL UP, ASSHOLE !!
uh...
WHAT'S GOING ON?!
IT'S A FIGHT!
UESUGI IS GETTING PUMMELED!
It cant be!
A...

ASS-HOLE?!
(ME? THIS SHINING EXAMPLE OF YOUNG BEAUTY?!)
KILL YOU
I'M GONNA KILL THAT PUNK!
IS THAT NORMAL, TO STALK SOME GUY WITH THE INTENT OF HAVING A MANLY ALTERCATION IN A DARK ALLEY?
SHUT UP, PEASANT. YOU'LL NEVER UNDERSTAND THE GRAVITY OF HIS CRIME.
Oh, no, Uesugi, don't die!
Take me with you!
Thank you, I love you...
What an idiot...
......
YAMADA
WHY AM I BEST FRIENDS WITH THIS GUY ANYWAY?
SO HE GOES HOME ALONE, EH? IT MUST BE BECAUSE HE HAS A BAD PERSONALITY AND NO FRIENDS.
DO YOU MEAN HIM OR YOU?
中央東口

WHY DO I HAVE TO COME ALONG, ANYWAY?
QUIT SNIVELING. YOU SHOULD BE HONORED TO BE MY CHAMPION.
HEY, LOOK! SHE'S MEGA HOT!
Yeah, she's okay...
DOES THIS MEAN WE HAVE TO SAY HELLO?
blush
WHAT?
WHAT? WHAT? WHAT?
SHE MUST BE HIS SISTER ...
WHAT SISTER WOULD GET DRESSED LIKE THAT FOR HER BROTHER? OR HOLD HIS HAND?
ahhh
uh
uh
uh
uh
uh

WHAT?! YOU CAN'T MEAN THAT DYNAMITE BABE IS DATING THAT SIMPERING FOOL?!
Explain yourself, mister!
Take that, dickhole!
THE ABILITY TO DEAL WITH REALITY IS A SIGN OF MATURITY.
I-I DON'T BELIEVE IT... HOW COULD SOMEONE SO BEAUTIFUL ...
WHY THAT LOSER? HE'S SHORTER, UGLIER, AND STUPIDER (THEORETICALLY) THAN I AM, YET HE'S MAKING THE SIGN OF THE TWO-HUMPED CAMEL (ALLEGEDLY) WITH THAT SEXY CHICK!
WHY, GOD, WHY?! IS IT TRENDY TO DATE TROLLS?!
.....
THAT-
THAT'S UNFORGIVABLE!!
UESUGI, WOULD YOU LIKE SOME BENTO?
TATSUYA DARLING!
EXCUSE ME, IS UESUGI HERE?
BABY-CAKES!

TOILET
HEY, YAMADA, WHERE'S YOUR BUDDY?
HM? ISN'T UESUGI AROUND?
Hey, some guys have all the luck!
UNO
Huh?
WHO KNOWS? MAYBE HE'S GETTING GANG RAPED IN THE BATHROOM.
MALE BONDING IS FUNNY.
Ha ha ha ha! What?!
THE KING

MAYBE I SHOULD JUST FORGET WHAT I SAW...

I WAS TIRED, AND I COULD HAVE BEEN HALLUCINATING.

I THINK I HAD A FEVER TOO. C'MON, SMILE, TATSUYA! BIG SMILE, MY SWEET BIRD OF YOUTH. SAY GOODBYE TO THAT SAD FACE!

OH, MAN... C'MON, HOT STUFF, SNAP OUT OF IT.

YOU'RE THE STAR OF THIS SCHOOL.

toilet

ALL EYES ARE ON YOU! THERE ARE MORE GIRLS WHO WANT YOU THAN STARS IN THE SKY!!

Damn it! I love me!!

In Use

...?

What's going on?

THAT SETTLES IT... NEXT TIME I SEE HIM I'M GONNA TEAR HIS CLOTHES OFF AND DROWN HIM IN THE RIVER...
...BUT BEFORE THAT I'M GONNA SHOVE HIM INTO THE GIRLS' BATHROOM. (grade school mentality)
YOU'RE STILL THE BEST! I LOVE YOU!
...
HE'S SICK.
YOUR PAL NEEDS AN INTER-VENTION.
Yamada
OKAY! MY EGO IS INTACT! LET'S EAT, YAMADA!
Time to roll!
I'm already eating, asswipe!
SO, SELF-HYPNOSIS IS THE KEY TO YOUR IRRATIONAL SELF-ABSORPTION, EH?
WHY EAT IN THE LIBRARY LIKE A HERMIT?
YOU DON'T UNDERSTAND THE JOY OF BEING ME, YAMADA.
HUH?

AAAAGH!
TATSUYA, IT'S THE GUY FROM YESTERDAY!
YOU'RE ...
YOU PUNY FRESHMAN...
...A GIRL...
HUH?
A GIRL?!

I'M REALLY SORRY ABOUT YESTERDAY!
I SHOULDN'T HAVE LOST MY TEMPER.
CLOSED
Lunch Break!! Do not Disturb!
I REALLY WANTED TO APOLOGIZE ...
I was waiting...
AND I HEARD YOU ALWAYS EAT IN THE LIBRARY, SO I WAS WAITING FOR YOU...
SO YOU'RE SOME KIND OF FEMME FATALE...
IT HONESTLY DOESN'T SHOW.
YEAH, MOST PEOPLE NEVER KNOW I'M A GIRL AT FIRST.
My voice is deep...
...and I have no breasts
DO YOU THINK DRESSING LIKE A DUDE HELPS?
Try a skirt...
I DUNNO, I GUESS IT'S A REACTION TO MY BROTHER'S STYLE...
REACTION?

IS YOUR BROTHER KIND OF GIRLISH?
A manly man knows how to cook!
Stereotype
BRO
Well, duh!
NOTHING WRONG WITH THAT, AS LONG AS HE COOKS AND CLEANS.
DON'T BE DUMB! HE JUST DRIVES ME NUTS THE WAY HE ACTS LIKE A CHILD.
LIKE YESTERDAY, HE WANTED ME TO GO SHOPPING WITH HIM AFTER SCHOOL.
AND HE WAS SO GIDDY, HE WANTED TO HOLD HANDS WITH ME.
I was mortified...

THERE YOU ARE, YUKIKO.
HELLO! ARE THESE YOUR FRIENDS?
Wow, what handsome guys...

I'M SURPRISED, REALLY...
I MEAN, YOU'RE QUITE LOVELY!
NO, NOT AT ALL...
tee hee hee
OH, STOP IT!
SHE'S NEVER BROUGHT BOYS HOME BEFORE.
SHE'S USUALLY MORE POPULAR WITH THE GIRLS.
Nothing like me...
OH, REALLY...
I'D STARTED TO WORRY ABOUT HER.
I WAS BEGINNING TO THINK SHE WAS A LESBIAN OR SOMETHING.
Gimme a break. You're one to talk...
Ha ha ha ha ha
I MEAN, WE'VE GROWN UP WITHOUT PARENTS, SO...
...WE'RE ALL THE FAMILY WE HAVE.

IT'S HARD ENOUGH TO HAVE A BROTHER LIKE ME, SO I DIDN'T WANT HER TO BE "DIFFERENT" AS WELL.
I MEAN, OUR PARENTS ARE PROBABLY TWIRLING IN THEIR GRAVES.
y'know?
SO YOU'D BETTER TAKE GOOD CARE OF MY SISTER, UESUGI-SAN...
WITH A MANLY VOICE
Chizuru
H-hey, man, don't scare me!
Don't be so mean to me!
Hey, you okay, Tatsuya?!
I ONLY WANTED TO APOLOGIZE FOR YESTERDAY.
I'M SORRY, MY BROTHER IS A LITTLE WEIRD...
He's in Love!
WHAT ARE YOU SAYING?! HE'S A GREAT BIG BROTHER!!
THNIC
ATIVE
MAY I HAVE PERMISSION TO BE PENPALS WITH YOUR BROTHER, YUKIKO?!
......

OH, DON'T GIVE YESTERDAY ANOTHER THOUGHT.
REALLY? BUT...
IT'S NO BIG DEAL...
IT WAS MY FAULT FOR NOT WATCHING WHERE I WAS GOING.
BESIDES, I CAN'T BE ANGRY AT A PRETTY YOUNG LADY...
Heh heh, total gentleman!
YOU'RE GOING STRAIGHT TO HELL SOMEDAY... You faker.
OKAY, WELL, I'M SORRY, NEVER-THELESS.
I'VE ALWAYS BEEN A REAL HOTHEAD.
CHIZURU IS ALWAYS TELLING ME TO BE MORE LADYLIKE.
IT'S SAD, BUT MY BROTHER IS PRETTIER AND MORE GIRLISH THAN ME.
......
ha ha ha. It's all backwards!
AS YOU CAN SEE, I'M KIND OF A FAILURE AS A SISTER. I'M SURE HE'S PRETTY DISAPPOINTED.
THAT'S NOT TRUE.

IN OTHER WORDS ...
HE WAS ACTUALLY HOPING WE COULD SET YOU STRAIGHT.
YOUR BROTHER'S JUST LOOKING OUT FOR YOU.
YUKIKO, LET'S BE FRIENDS, OKAY?
HUH... ?
WHAT? UH...
S-
SURE.
THAT'S COOL...
I GUESS ...
KIRSTEN DUNST AND ALYSON HANNIGAN AND PARKER POSEY...
WHO ELSE?
にやにやにや
← chopsticks
THAT'S A PRETTY IDEAL PROTOTYPE, PRETTY BOY.
y'know?
WELL, AN IDEAL IS USUALLY FAR FROM REALITY.
THAT'S A BOLD STATEMENT FOR YOU.
Reality is your enemy.

SOMETIMES AN ECCENTRIC GIRL CAN BE REFRESHING.
COME ON, YOU KNOW WHAT I MEAN...
どたどた どたどた どた
E- ECCENTRIC?
Huh?
どど たっ
UESUGI! IT'S LUNCH TIME!!
C'MON!!
WHAT ARE YOU WAITING FOR?! AREN'T WE FRIENDS?! GET ME SOME DAMN TEA!!
アンネの日記
ボコッ
She's pretty wild!
I CAN'T THINK OF ANY TWO PEOPLE MORE DIFFERENT THAN YOU AND I...
...BUT OPPOSITES ATTRACT, AND ADVENTURE IS REFRESHING.
Life is a one-way ticket, y'know? (whatever that means.)
I BARELY RECOGNIZE YOU AS THE GUY FROM THE START OF THIS STORY.
HA HA HA HA! I FEEL FOR YOUR SANITY! I WISH I COULD SHARE SOME OF MY HAPPINESS WITH YOU!
はっはっは
Goddammit!
YOU'RE FEELING PRETTY SMUG, AREN'T YOU, YOU BASTARD?!
oh my
Oh. I HEARD YAMADA IS SHARING A DIARY WITH MY BRO.
I GUESS IT'S A MERE TEA-SPOON OF HAPPINESS, AFTER ALL...
Yamada

BUT I WOULD ASSUME YOUR FANS AREN'T GOING TO STAY QUIET ABOUT THIS.
Uesugi, you're so cool!
I'M SURE SHE'LL COME TO UNDERSTAND ...
YOU'RE PROBABLY RIGHT.
I'm such a cad!
Look this way!
Eeeeek!
...HOW BIG A DEAL IT IS THAT I'M IN LOVE.
HEY, WHAT ARE YOU TWO TALKING ABOUT?!
We're buddies, right?! Tell me what's going on!
SHOW ME SOME LINGERIE AND I'LL REVEAL ALL!
Forget it!
BUT...
I HEARD UESUGI IS DATING A FRESHMAN!
WHAT?! NO WAY!!
What bitch is that?!
BUT IT'S NOT A GIRL, IT'S A GUY!
YOWZA!
FORBIDDEN LOVE!!
Sounds kinky!
I CAN GO FOR THAT!
Me, too! Go for it, Uesugi!
LITTLE DID THEY KNOW THE TRAGEDY THAT THIS MIS-UNDERSTANDING WOULD BEAR UPON THEM...

Gravitation

Blow a Yakuza job and cut off a finger? (ouch!)
Lead Bad Luck in a sold-out concert to promote our new album!
Eat the legendary Gum Gum fruit and become King of the Pirates?
Crash Woodstock 2 with Sakuma?
Find out about the Donnie Darko world of Nittle Grasper's lead singer?
Spend a little quality time with the Japanese Alex Trebec?
クイズでポーイ!
QUIZ DE PON!
Shuichi's Things to do in Volume 3...

ALSO AVAILABLE FROM TOKYOPOP®

SAMURAI DEEPER KYO
SAMURAI GIRL REAL BOUT HIGH SCHOOL
SCRYED
SEIKAI TRILOGY, THE CREST OF THE STARS
SGT. FROG
SHAOLIN SISTERS
SHIRAHIME-SYO: SNOW GODDESS TALES
SHUTTERBOX
SKULL MAN, THE
SNOW DROP
SOKORA REFUGEES
SORCERER HUNTERS
SUIKODEN III
SUKI
TOKYO BABYLON
TOKYO MEW MEW
UNDER THE GLASS MOON
VAMPIRE GAME
VISION OF ESCAFLOWNE, THE
WILD ACT
WISH
WORLD OF HARTZ
X-DAY
ZODIAC P.I.

NOVELS

KARMA CLUB
SAILOR MOON

ART BOOKS

COWBOY BEBOP ANIME GUIDES
GUNDAM TECHNICAL MANUALS
SAILOR MOON SCOUT GUIDES

ANIME GUIDES

COWBOY BEBOP ANIME GUIDES
GUNDAM TECHNICAL MANUALS
SAILOR MOON SCOUT GUIDES

TOKYOPOP KIDS

STRAY SHEEP

CINE-MANGA™

CARDCAPTORS
FAIRLY ODDPARENTS, THE
FINDING NEMO
G.I. JOE SPY TROOPS
JACKIE CHAN ADVENTURES
JIMMY NEUTRON BOY GENIUS, THE ADVENTURES OF
KIM POSSIBLE
LIZZIE MCGUIRE
POWER RANGERS: NINJA STORM
SPONGEBOB SQUAREPANTS
SPY KIDS 2
SPY KIDS 3-D: GAME OVER
TRANSFORMERS: ARMADA
TRANSFORMERS: ENERGON

For more information visit www.TOKYOPOP.com

12.20.03T

STOP!

This is the back of the book. You wouldn't want to spoil a great ending!

This book is printed "manga-style," in the authentic Japanese right-to-left format. Since none of the artwork has been flipped or altered, readers get to experience the story just as the creator intended. You've been asking for it, so TOKYOPOP® delivered: authentic, hot-off-the-press, and far more fun!

DIRECTIONS

If this is your first time reading manga-style, here's a quick guide to help you understand how it works.

It's easy... just start in the top right panel and follow the numbers. Have fun, and look for more 100% authentic manga from TOKYOPOP®!